1st Battalion
The Wiltshire Regiment
in the
Great War

A commentary and analysis of their War Diary

Edwin Astill

For Troy

and in memory of my parents

Harry and Barbara Astill

Published by

RGBW (Salisbury) Museum
58 The Close
Salisbury
Wiltshire
SP1 2EX

Telephone : (01722) 419419
Website : www.thewardrobe.org.uk

Registered as a Charity (number 272051)

ISBN 0-9540365-4-9

Contents

Maps

1st Battalion The Wiltshire Regiment in the Great War

A commentary and analysis of their War Diary

"By their Deeds shall thee know them".

Introduction

This reference to Matthew's Gospel (Mt. 7:20) was written at the end of the diary entry for 14th August 1914, at Rouen - the battalion's first day on French soil. It follows an appendix listing the 25 officers present then. The diarist clearly knew that momentous days were ahead. In fact, over 4 years of active service were to follow which would see the battalion employ over 300 officers at various stages. Their deeds have immortalised them and their comrades in the British Expeditionary Force. The Great War still generates interest, debate, and admiration for the men taking part.

The website of The Royal Gloucestershire, Berkshire and Wiltshire Museum (www.thewardrobe.org.uk) enables visitors to access the war diaries of those Regiments whose memories it seeks to preserve. This prompted me to undertake a piece of research that has given me much pleasure over the past year or more. It has helped dispel in my own mind those myths upon which my generation were fed and which are now - alas! - still widespread. Naturally many men came away from the war angry and embittered by what they had been through, but many more (including my grandfather, Sapper (later Major) Frank Astill, R.E.) saw the war as a duty to be done. They were quietly proud of the part they played. Modern historians are now putting the war into perspective. So powerful has been the influence of the 'war poets' (an essential component of any school literature syllabus) and others that it has taken nearly three quarters of a century for this to come about.

Although several excellent books cover the history of the Wiltshire Regiment none give a detailed account of the 1st Wilts during the Great War. At the time of writing it seems that the county name will disappear completely from the roll of our nation's regiments – all the more reason to acknowledge the debt we owe to the brave men who answered their country's call and fought under the colours of the Wiltshire Regiment.

Parts of the War Diary have been used by both the *Official History* and other published accounts of the war. However, there is still much information in it that tells us about daily life at the front and out of line. It adds detail to the broad canvass that can be followed in the history books. By narrowing on topics we can detect the evolution of the army from its original form at Mons to the complex organisation it became in the latter part of the War. The War Diary has been used in conjunction with the list of officer casualties as supplied by the Museum.

Appendix A gives the instructions relating to the composition of War Diaries. The War Diaries for the 1/Wilts cover most of the aspects required by the instructions at one time or other, although it is noticeable that the quality and content of entries varies, perhaps due to the demands of active service, but also because of the individual styles of the officers compiling them. Even some of the extraneous items - the results of inter-battalion football matches - serve to add colour and interest to the diaries, even if the content did not strictly comply with the official instructions. The War Diaries are not complete, with a tendency for entries to be skipped as the war progressed. In many cases single entries were made to cover 'missing' days.

Part of this work is a narrative history of the battalion, derived from the War Diary and augmented from other sources to complete the detail. The second section is a summary of three diaries or accounts kept by individual members of the battalion (and now held in the Imperial War Museum Collection). The final part looks at particular topics, again derived from the War Diary, but also using the detail from the officer casualty list.

The appendices include a Gazetteer of places occupied by the 1/Wilts during the war. I hope this will help readers identify locations on maps, and perhaps encourage them to visit the sites. A feel for the topography greatly assists an understanding of the actions.

Although some maps have been included, it is helpful to have a large-scale map to hand when reading this work or the War Diary. The Michelin Local 1:150,000 series is easily obtainable and useful for this purpose.

Finally, recognition and thanks must be paid to all those who have helped me in compiling this work. In particular:

My brother, Dr. John Astill, for his helpful comments and suggestions.

The Brotherton Library (Special Collections) Leeds University for permission to use the writings of Capt. G.K. Wait and Lt. A.J.S. White held in the Liddle Collection. Thanks are particularly owed to the library staff for their help.

The Trustees and staff of the Imperial War Museum for their assistance and help in tracking down material, and for advice on copyright holders. Material by J.L. Mohan, H.G. Perry and Lt. R. Swayne is held by the Museum. Every effort has been made to contact the copyright holders but this has not been possible.

David Chilton and the staff at the Royal Gloucestershire, Berkshire and Wiltshire Regiment Museum, Salisbury, for making available the War Diary, Officer Casualty lists, photographs, and for their support generally.

Permission to use material has kindly been given by:

Mr Hugh Andrew - George Macklin's quotes, from David Ascoli's 'The Mons Star'.

Mr. Anthony M. Gaskell for extracts from his father's work 'My Experiences in 1914' (held in the Imperial War Museum collection).

The Worcestershire Regiment Museum Trust for extracts from the diary of Col. A.C. Johnston.

The Royal Ulster Rifles Association for material from Cyril Falls' book on the Royal Irish Rifles in the Great War.

Attempts to track down other copyright holders have been unsuccessful, although all sources have been acknowledged.

The database of the Commonwealth War Graves Commission (http://www.cwgc.org) has been an invaluable tool in checking details of those killed in action.

Edwin Astill

Sheffield 2005

Part 1 - 1/Wilts - Brief History

Chapter 1 - 1914 - The Opening Battles

Mobilization

At 5.45p.m. on Tuesday, 4th August 1914, orders to mobilize were received by the battalion. Earlier that day the German army had invaded Belgium; on the previous day Germany had declared war on France. The British ultimatum to Germany expired at 11p.m., 5¼ hours after the mobilization order had been received by 1/Wilts at Tidworth, and 6½ hours after the order had been issued. In just 4 days the battalion was able to report to brigade that mobilization was complete. The next 4 days were spent in musketry practice, route marches, medicals, and in tidying up loose ends, including the settling of accounts. And so, early in the morning of 13th August 1914, the whole battalion was ready to entrain for Southampton where they would board 2 ships bound for France.

The War Diary suggests all went smoothly - and so it did for the British Expeditionary Force (B.E.F.) as a whole. The War Book laid down in minute detail the steps that were to be followed. The main task was in getting the battalion up to strength with its reserves, kitting out the men, and making sure that all the equipment needed to maintain over 1,000 men in the field was ready. As can be imagined, the real story would have been one of frantic effort by all concerned. Not recorded in the diary was the problem the Quartermaster had in finding sufficient boots size 10 and 11 for those rejoining the colours.[1]

Embarkation also had its problems, the hatches of the steam ships being too small for the G.S.[2] wagons. This meant having to take off shafts and wheels. Both halves of the battalion sailed for France, disembarked at Rouen, and then marched to camp at Mont St.Aignan (some 3 miles north of Rouen).

The 1/Wilts formed part of II Corps (Lt. Gen. Sir H. Smith-Dorrien), 3rd Division (Maj. Gen. H. Hamilton), 7th Infantry Brigade (Brig. Gen. F. McCracken). In 1914 an infantry brigade consisted of 4 battalions: the others

---

1 *Ascoli, The Mons Star, Ch. 2.*

2 *General Service.*

in 7th Brigade being the 3/Worcesters, 2/South Lancs and 2/Royal Irish Rifles. (See Appendix B for details of the formations throughout the war.)

Mont St. Aignan - Mons - the Marne

Once in France the B.E.F.'s purpose was, according to Kitchener's instructions to the Commander-in Chief:

> … to support and co-operate with the French Army in preventing or repelling the invasion by Germany of French and Belgian territory and eventually to restore the neutrality of Belgium.

To this end the B.E.F. was to go to Mons, on the left flank of the French armies, and advance in support of the planned advance of their allies. The 16th August saw the battalion make an early start, entraining at Rouen for a journey northeast to Aulnoye (Aulnoye-Aymeries) some 20 or so miles south of Mons. This journey took around 16 hours. For the next 4 days they were based at Marbaix (a little to the south of Aulnoye), where they rested, took up guard duties, and enjoyed a route march to Avesnes, where they were fêted by locals. On 20th August the Commander-in-Chief, Sir John French, ordered an advance of the whole force north of the River Sambre and accordingly, on the following day, the 1/Wilts marched north to Feignies, just a mile or so west of the fortress town of Maubeuge. A shorter march the next day brought the battalion to Ciply/Harmignies/Nouvelles. On Sunday, 23rd August they were ordered to entrench north of Ciply, and came under enemy artillery fire for the first time. The greater part of 3rd Division were ahead, with 7th Brigade acting as reserve, with 1/Wilts acting as brigade reserve just over ½ mile south of Ciply. The first battle was on.

Whilst this was happening the German *First Army* (Kluck) was spotted by British aerial reconnaissance on 22nd August. It was wheeling towards Mons in order to close the gap between it and the *Second Army*. During the course of the day it became apparent that the B.E.F. was facing a substantial enemy force, and that the proposed French advance on their right flank would not take place: quite the reverse, the French were to retreat. A request from the French to attack the German Second Army was out of the question, although Sir John French agreed to stay put for 24 hours. II Corps took up its defensive position along the Canal running West-East past Mons. After a day of stiff fighting II Corps retreated to higher ground south of the canal.

By 24th August the Germans were across the Canal, and attacking positions Frameries-Ciply. McCracken's 7th Brigade was ordered to retire and some time after 9a.m., and with some difficulty, they did so. The 2/S. Lancs acted as rearguard, although 1/Wilts would be the last the leave. The War Diary records the first fatalities - Captain Dawes and 3 men, with the Adjutant (Capt. Rowan) wounded along with 20 men. The C.O.'s horse was also a casualty. The 3rd Division ended the day occupying a line St Waast-Amfroipret-Bermeries. The retreat was on. Map 1 shows the route taken during the early stages of the campaign.

A tribute to the work of 1/Wilts and their brigade was earned from Lt. Gen. Smith-Dorrien, who writing his memoirs[3] some time later said:

> "The Brigade of II Corps on rear-guard was McCracken's, the 7th, and so well were they handled and so brilliantly did the two Battalions engaged (the South Lancashires and the Wiltshires) conduct themselves, that in consequence of a recommendation of General Allenby's, endorsed by the C.-in-C, their Brigadier was promoted Major-General."[4]

On the following day (25th August) the 7th Infantry Brigade retired to Gommignies, but was driven out by the enemy. They continued their march to Caudry via Le Quesnoy and Solesmes. At a position just a mile or so north of Solesmes, at 5.45p.m., 1/Wilts and 2/S.Lancs halted and deployed. By 6p.m. they were the only units covering the road to Solesmes, and they were heavily engaged by the enemy. They held out until dusk, when the Germans went into bivouac. This enabled the two battalions to continue their movement on Caudry. Fortunately they were not pursued during this night-time march. Even without the fighting, the congested roads, and the hot August weather, the battalion had covered an exhausting and almost unbelievable 40 miles since leaving Ciply at 1p.m.[5] the day before. The rearguard of 3rd Division did not make it to Caudry until around midnight. Some elements of 1/Wilts became detached and ended up at Le Cateau, having avoided capture with difficulty.

---

3 *Memories of Forty-Eight Years Service.*

4 *McCracken was appointed Major General and commanded the 15th (Scottish) Division from March 1915 to June 1917, when he was promoted Lieutenant General in command of a Corps. He died in 1949.*

5 *Military Operations 1914 Vol 1 puts the time of departure sometime shortly after 9am on 24 August.*

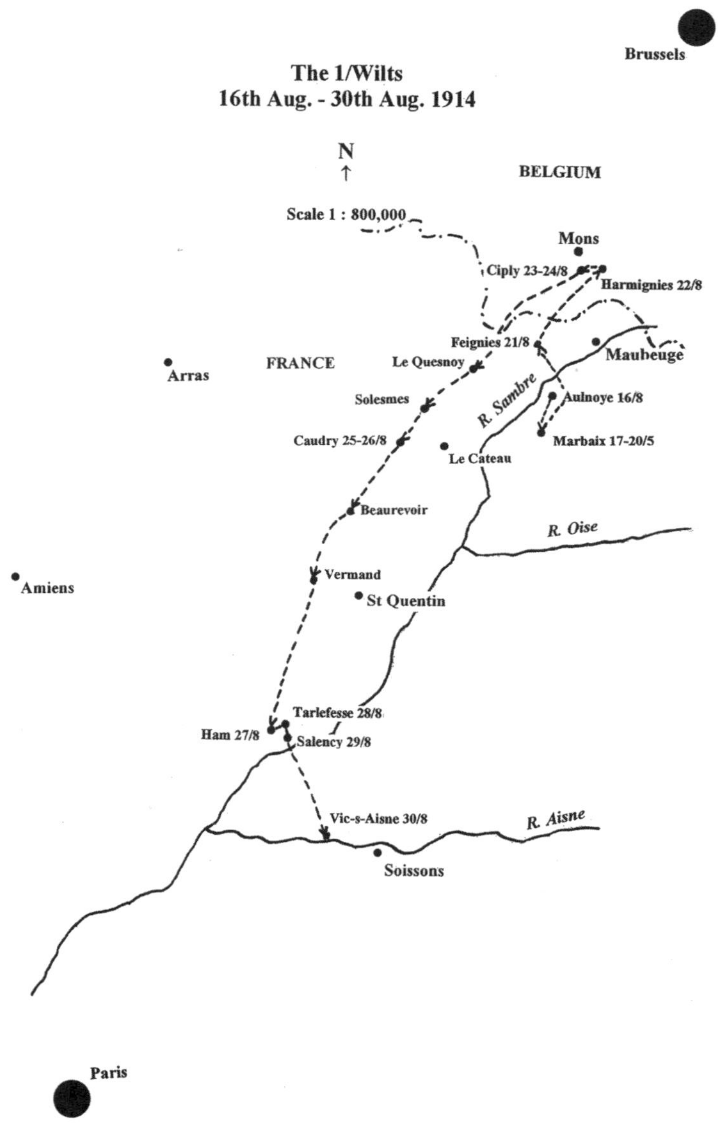
Brussels
The 1/Wilts
16th Aug. - 30th Aug. 1914
N
BELGIUM
Scale 1 : 800,000
Mons
Ciply 23-24/8
Harmignies 22/8
Feignies 21/8
Maubeuge
Arras
FRANCE
Le Quesnoy
Solesmes
R. Sambre
Aulnoye 16/8
Caudry 25-26/8
Le Cateau
Marbaix 17-20/5
Beaurevoir
R. Oise
Vermand
Amiens
St Quentin
Tarlefesse 28/8
Ham 27/8
Salency 29/8
Vic-s-Aisne 30/8
R. Aisne
Soissons
Paris

Map 1

The rest of II Corps had to cover a similar distance, and consequently the Corps Commander, Gen. Smith-Dorrien, felt unable to continue the retirement without endangering his command. In reaching this decision he had consulted with other commanders at around 2a.m. on 26th. August. They convinced him that none of the units were in a fit state to continue the retirement that night. Maj. Gen. Hamilton for one felt that 3rd Division could not move before 9.a.m. that morning. Smith-Dorrien, with the co-operation of Allenby's Cavalry Division and Maj. Gen. Snow's incomplete 4th Division, determined to make at stand on the line Le Cateau-Caudry-Esnes. The 3rd Division was in the centre of this line, at Caudry, with 4th Division to the left and 5th Division to the right. The 1/Wilts held a position on a ridge just to the north east of the town, on the right flank of 7th Brigade. The main German attack was on the flanks of the British position, and so the centre was less severely affected. Even so, they had a stiff fight on their hands, being shelled and attacked by infantry. The War Diary for 26th August records casualties of between 80-100. The retreat of 3rd Division was effected smoothly, although in this the forces at Le Cateau were helped by the rearguard actions of the Gordon Highlanders and the Royal Scots, who did not receive the order to retreat in time.

The retreat continued, largely unhampered by the Germans. From 27th August until 5th September the War Diary records the places passed through and the nightly billets. In *'The Story of the Wiltshire Regiment'* [6] it is stated that the C.O. (Lt. Col. Hasted) had become separated from his command whilst trying to coordinate its (by now) mixed up components. The only contact with the enemy occurred on 31st August, when outposts of 'B' Company exchanged shots with an 'Uhlan patrol'. Other activity noted includes the demolition of bridges and providing guard for the army. The *Official History* notes that 3rd Division missed their supply column, and were without rations from 25th August until the afternoon of 27th August. Map 2 shows the route of the later stages of the retreat and the advance to the River Aisne.

6 *Chapter XIII - The 1st Battalion. By Col. N. C. E. Kenrick, Published by Gale & Polden 1963.*

The 1/Wilts
30th Aug - 5th October 1914

N
↑

Scale 1:460,000

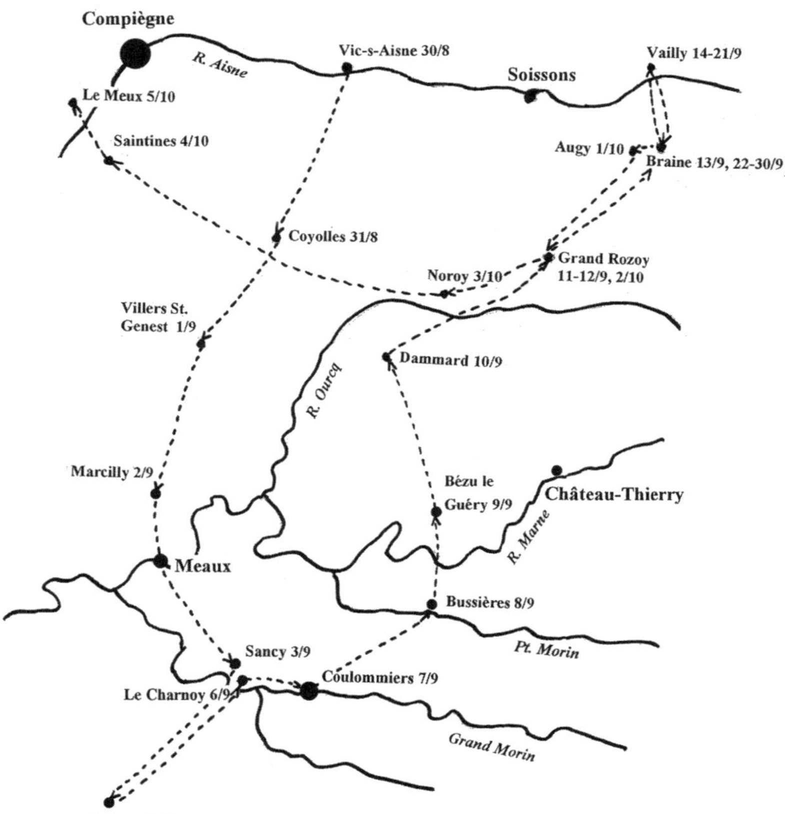

Map 2

In all 1/Wilts had marched at least 220 miles since arriving at Aulnoye Station. The men were tired but not defeated. George Macklin of the 1/Wilts recorded[7]

> We had lost count of the days. All we knew was that we had come to France to fight. Now for no reason we were told the retreat would go on. Just that. No one told us why. We had lost a lot of our pals, but we hadn't expected a tea-party. It was back to the road and the dust and the heat and never a German in sight. No wonder we felt bloody-minded.

Appendix C gives the route and distances taken during the retreat.

On 5th September a party of reinforcements reached the battalion - one officer and 89 rank and file. Higher up the French chain of command it became apparent by 3rd September that Kluck's *First Army* had wheeled to the east of Paris, thereby offering a flank to the French forces to the west of the B.E.F., and to the B.E.F. itself. Early on the morning of 5th September a copy of Joffre's (French C-in-C) Instruction No. 6 reached the B.E.F.'s G.H.Q. This pointed to the offensive starting on 6th September, the B.E.F. acting in concert with the French armies on either flank. The aim was to deliver a blow to the right flank of the German forces. These instructions arrived too late to halt the British retirement, which further separated itself from its French allies. It took a personal visit to the British G.H.Q. by Joffre to persuade Sir John French to halt the British retreat, turn it about, and to cooperate with their allies. The retreat was over.

The Aisne

And so, on 6th September, the War Diary notes - perhaps with relief - that "The advance north commenced." This day was to see 1/Wilts earn another important place in military history. The 3rd Division pushed forward to the Grand Morin (a tributary of the River Marne) at Faremoutiers, with 1/Wilts taking advantage of weak opposition and making the river crossing before occupying the high ground at Le Charnois, some mile of so further north. George Macklin's mood changed:[8]

---

7 *Quoted in David Ascoli's 'The Mons Star' Chap. 7*

8 *From Ascoli, op. cit.*

> First in at Mons and now first of the hunting pack! There had been a bit of a scrap while we were waiting to cross and I got a slight wound in the hand. But we were soon over and up the slope the other side. It was a moonlight night and we could see a few Germans scurrying away. We put out our picquets and settled down, feeling pretty pleased with ourselves. Then I clearly remember someone started singing 'You are my honeysuckle, I am the bee!' and everybody began laughing. Nothing strange about that until I realized it was a long time since we had anything to laugh about. After that I slept like a log.

The Wiltshires were the advance guard of the brigade, and the brigade headed the division. Their pressing forward was brisk, but unfortunately the rest of the B.E.F. were not so far forward, and an opportunity was missed to deliver a more serious blow to the enemy. On the 7th September the battalion spent time retiring back to Faremoutiers before moving forward to Coulommiers (in fact moving in an eastward direction), where they were reinforced by a further 90 men under an officer. During the day, according to the *Official History*, approximately 200 dismounted men of the German *Guards Cavalry Division* attacked the1/Wilts at 6 a.m. The enemy were beaten off without difficulty.

The next day, 8th September, marked a further step forward, with 1/Wilts reaching Bussiques (Bussières) at dusk. The advance of 6 miles started at 7a.m., and was held up until the 8th Brigade drove out enemy opposition at Orly (a village a mile of so south east of Bussiques). A further short march the following day took the 1/Wilts directly north of Bézu-le-Guery, via Nanteuil, where the Marne crossing was made. Here the bridges were found to be intact. A delay on this day was caused by the enemy's command of the road with his artillery. A diversion via some woods enabled the advance to continue, whilst the Lincolnshire Regiment neutralised the German guns.

By this time the German *First* and *Second Armies* were given definite orders to retire to the Aisne. So, by the night of the 9th September, the German right wing was committed to a full-scale retreat. On the 10th September, after glorious weather since arriving in France, the B.E.F. was faced with rain that slowed down their pursuit. The War Diary fails to note this point, but does record that the 3rd Division captured some 500-600 prisoners. The bad weather was recorded on the 11th where the men spent a miserable night with little shelter at Grand Rozoy. By midnight of 12th September, the B.E.F. crossed the River Vesle - outposts of the 1/Wilts arriving at Braine. A day's delay was encountered as the Germans had destroyed the bridges across the Aisne. The Royal Engineers had put a number of bridges across the Aisne, and this enabled part of 3rd Division (8th and 9th Brigades) to cross on the night of 13th /14th September. At daybreak on the 14th the 1/Wilts were required to support these brigades who were being engaged by the enemy. Hostile artillery fire prevented them from using the most convenient bridge, but under cover of woods they were able to make for the railway bridge between Vailly and Presles. Wooden planks across this partially destroyed bridge had made it usable. However, on reaching the railway bridge they met part of the 9th Brigade who were falling back. The battalion covered their retirement, and a little later, under the command of Lt. Col. Bird of the Royal Irish Rifles, the troops in the area re-crossed the Aisne and took up positions on the hills on the north bank. Here they entrenched, and beat off a half-hearted attack by the enemy at 11p.m.

The 1/Wilts were to spend the next 9 days at Vailly. The War Diary notes the daily pattern of shelling, patrols, and attacks. The most serious of these occurred on 20th September, when an enemy group of about 200 with machine guns were able to penetrate dense woodland and attack the Worcester's rear flanks. Severe hand-to-hand fighting took place, and an enemy break through seemed possible until artillery fire was brought to bear upon them. The Brigadier was also obliged to call upon the 4th Guards Brigade to assist. Throughout, 3 companies of the Wiltshires continued to hold the enemy at bay. By 5.45 p.m. the original lines were regained, following an attack by a force gathered from the 7th Brigade. The whole engagement was carried out at some loss to the battalion - the C.O., Lt Col. Hasted wounded (his place being taken by Maj. Roche), and 3 officers killed (2/Lt. Cruickshank, Capt. Renolds and 2/Lt. Roseveare). 2/Lt. Gaskell's diary gives an account of this action (see Part 2 - Three Personal Diaries) and subsequent events.

The following day saw the arrival of 2 new machine guns to replace those lost on 26th August near Le Cateau. Not so welcome from the diarist's point of view was the apparent jumpiness of the men, who kept up a fusillade during the night in response to enemy long distance fire. "This wild firing at night badly wants checking and discouraging."

Finally, the battalion moved into billets at Braine (some 3½ miles behind the front line) after being relieved by the Norfolk Regt. Movement across the Aisne was restricted to the hours of darkness due to enemy artillery. At Braine, on 24th September, they were visited and complimented upon by the Corps Commander, Lt. Gen. Sir Horace Smith Dorrien. The battalion was further reinforced and had time to reflect on its position, particularly regarding losses. The action over the past few days on the Aisne had cost them 160 casualties. Since arriving in France some 40 days earlier, 12 offices and 362 other ranks were killed, wounded or missing. The arithmetic in the War Diary is a little shaky, and even so there was a "difference of about 75 rank and file" which "I think made up by men gone sick and otherwise have dropped out."

From 24th-26th September the 1/Wilts rested and reorganised - their strength being brought up almost to full establishment (22 officers, 922 other ranks). During this period Major Barnes was ordered to Base,[9] and Capt. Rowan, Adjutant, rejoined the battalion after recovering from a wound received at Ciply. Over the days that followed some trench digging was undertaken at Brenelle, just a mile or so north of Braine, and a rumour of a German advance across the Aisne led to the Wiltshires being rushed to Chassemy.

On 1st October the battalion moved away from the Aisne, swinging in a semi-circle westward to Santines railway station, marching via Augy, Grand Rezoy, Noroy and Le Meux. Here they entrained for Abbeville. Attempts to break the Germans on the Aisne had failed, and both sides were looking to exploit the gap between the opposing armies and the English Channel. The first chapter was over.

Actions around Neuve Chapelle, October 1914

After reaching Abbeville the battalion were billeted at La Triquerie, just a few miles further north of the town. At the same time the Royal Naval Division at Antwerp was escaping from the German forces tasked with destroying the Belgian forts and armies. The left flank of the allies' line, near the coast, contained a mix of the newly arrived British troops under Gen. Rawlinson (including the 7th Division with the 2/Wilts), the retreating Belgian Army, as well as French forces.

On the evening of 8th October Sir John French ordered Sir Horace Smith-Dorrien to move II Corps east to St. Pol - Fruges. Motor transport was provided for the following day (its first mention in the War Diary, and a novelty perhaps for some of the men). By 12th October the battalion, with the rest of the B.E.F., had moved further north east. The B.E.F. occupied a line from Bethune - Hazebrouck - St. Omer, with Rawlinson's separate force, with

9 *According to the Officer Casualty list he had a "Special appointment from 16.8.1914, graded for the purposes of pay as a Staff Captain (London Gazette of 15.10.1915)." He returned to England on 6th October 1914.*

the Belgians, around Ghent. Whilst at La Couture, 5 miles north east of Bethune, the Brigade engaged the enemy, with 1/Wilts filling in gaps along the line and acting as escort for the Royal Field Artillery. They stayed here for 4 nights after beating off the Germans. Then, on the 16th, they moved to Neuve Chapelle, before spending a further 4 nights at Ligny-le-Grand. Their stay at Ligny was marked by constant sniping and shelling, and at night the enemy's use of star shells, searchlights, and the burning of hayricks restricted their movements. Map 3 shows the area of operations.

It was on the night of 18th/19th October that Pte. Tanner deserted, a deed for which he was later 'shot at dawn'.[10]

A lodgement was made in enemy positions at Illies on 19th October, but this could not be effectively exploited. The officers concerned (2/Lts Lloyd and Rose) therefore withdrew. Two days later the Germans broke the line to the right of the 7th Brigade, although the 1/Wilts and their comrades held their line. The *Official History*[11] describes the events as follows:

> About 7a.m. on the 21st, under cover of the mist, the Germans attacked, particularly the front of the 7th and 9th Brigades, between Le Transloy and Herlies. They surprised the left company of the 2/S.Lancashire (the right of the 7th Brigade), and having thus made an entry forced back the rest of the battalion and two companies of the 3/Worcestershire on its left. They then endeavoured to extend the gap; but the troops on its flanks - on the south the 1/Cornwall LI (14th Brigade), and on the north a company of the Worcestershire, with the battalion machine guns, the 1/Wiltshire and 2/Royal Irish Rifles - held on unflinchingly.

According to the War Diary the Germans attacked the 1/Wilts position before Haplegarde at about 6p.m. on the 21st, as 'B' Company moved off to start digging new positions. The attack was beaten off. At 2.30 a.m. on 22nd the Germans again attacked and surrounded 'D' Company, who held on until the attack failed an hour later. At 4.10 a.m. the 1/Wilts took up new positions south east of Haplegarde which proved untenable, and so they moved (at midnight, 22nd/23rd October) back to positions partially prepared by the Royal Engineers, west of Neuve Chapelle. The struggle had been unequal,

---

10 *The account given in 'Shot at Dawn' is discussed at Appendix D.*

11 *Military Operations France & Belgium 1914 Vol. II.*

with 11 German battalions pitted against the 4 British between Herlies and Illies.

At Neuve Chapelle the men got down to the business of making their position 'bomb-proof', although sniping made them defer this work until after nightfall. At 12.30 a.m. on the 24th their new position was again attacked for some 2 hours. At its conclusion the work on defences continued. Once daylight came the German artillery took over, and shelled the position for most of the day (although they had a couple of hours respite for lunch). Throughout these days (and the days to follow) there was a steady trickle of casualties. For the first time it was reported that many of the missing men were thought to have been buried in their dugouts. Heavy shelling continued on the following day, destroying the village and roads, and causing casualties.

By 26th October the battle became intense. At 1p.m. the position was subjected to very heavy shelling, and later the regiment to their left were almost cleared out of their trenches by the enemy. By 4.30 in the afternoon the Germans were working their way into the left of the Wilts' position. This infiltration was checked, and as dusk fell the enemy began to entrench themselves within 200 yards. A bayonet charge by 3 platoons of 'C' Company removed them and sent them retreating towards the now burning village. Reinforcements from within the 7th Brigade were promised for that night, with the intention of ousting the Germans from Neuve Chapelle. The Adjutant, Capt. P. S. Rowan, led a group of 5 companies from 3 regiments forward, 'C' Company of 1/Wilts leading the way. There were few Germans in the village apart from some snipers, but the enemy did occupy the Royal Irish Rifles' former trenches. Another bayonet encounter drove them off, and the trenches were reoccupied until further units of the R. Irish Rifles could be brought forward to relieve them. However, Germans were still in trenches to the north of the village, and the C.O. 1/Wilts (Maj. Roche) was all for removing them. By then more senior officers had arrived on the scene, and in view of the enemy artillery fire they decided to delay until the morning when their own artillery could be used to support the move. The 1/Wilts re-positioned, reinforced their positions, and re-supplied them. Cyril Falls' work[12] noted that "South East of the village their (2/R. Irish Rifles) splendid colleagues of the Wiltshire had clung to their trenches even when the enemy was behind them."

---

12 *'The Royal Irish Rifles in the Great War.'*

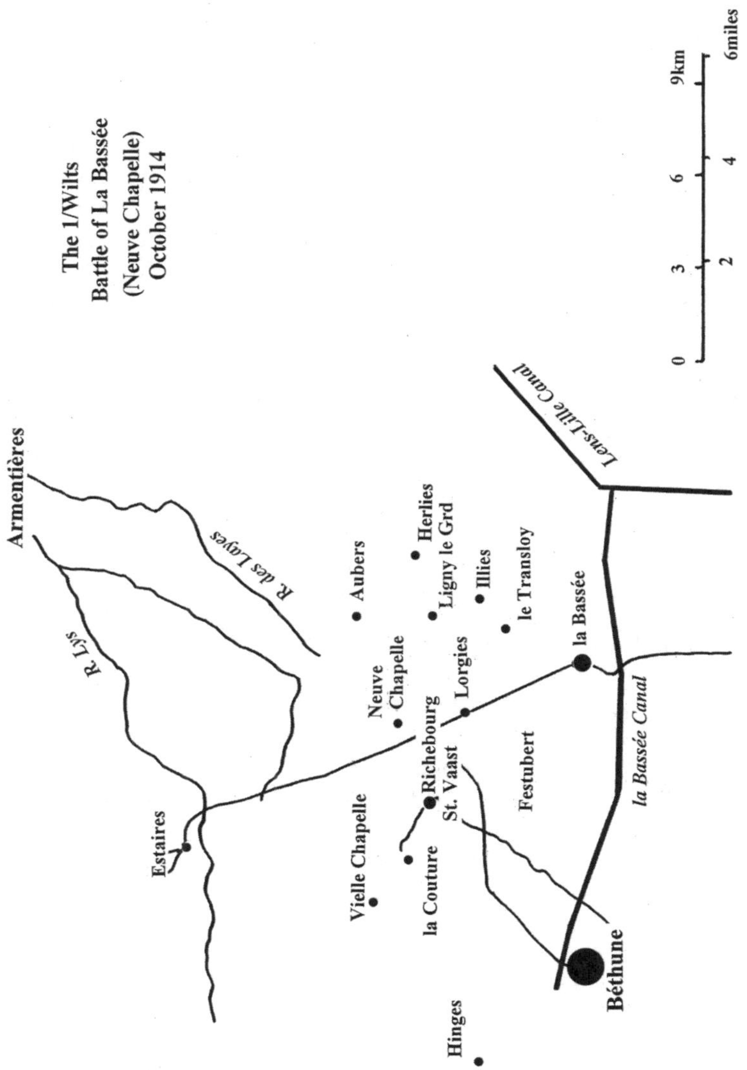
The 1/Wilts
Battle of La Bassée
(Neuve Chapelle)
October 1914
Armentières
R. des Layes
R. Lys
Estaires
Aubers
Herlies
Ligny le Grd
Illies
le Transloy
la Bassée
Neuve Chapelle
Lorgies
Richebourg
St. Vaast
Festubert
Vielle Chapelle
la Couture
Béthune
Hinges
la Bassée Canal
Lens-Lille Canal
0
3
6
9km
2
4
6miles

Map 3

The following day did not bring the expected reinforcements to assist in the attack, but at daybreak[13] the battalion found their position surrounded by snipers. Communications with the brigade were by runner, and eventually Lt. Goodheart got through to them with a message. Later in the morning a weak force of the S. Lancs came to the battalion's assistance, but only after it became clear that the 2/R. Irish Rifles had been forced out of their position.[14] The situation of the 1/Wilts was becoming very uncomfortable, but Brigade promised a strong attack on the village at 11a.m.[15] This attack materialised at midday, but did not make much progress. A message reporting a massing of enemy troops on the battalion's left failed to get through, although at 3.30 p.m. retreating British soldiers were observed, and they were being pursued by Germans. Those men at the battalion H.Q. - a mixed force of Wiltshiremen and S.Lancs - engaged with the enemy, who gave up the pursuit. However, the Germans re-grouped and attacked the H.Q. position. The attack was checked, although the 1/Wilts were exposed on their right flank. Bad news came through at 4p.m., when 2/Lt. Chandler reported that the left flank (held by the 2/R. Irish Rifles) had been broken. The battalion's untenable position was communicated to brigade, who promised assistance in the form of the 47th Sikhs.[16] Meanwhile the battalion should counter attack. Maj. Roche was clearly sceptical as to the chances of a counter attack succeeding, but agreed to hang on "and see what can be done when 47th Sikhs arrive". More confusion followed, with a Divisional staff officer saying that Sikhs had gone elsewhere, but that the 9th Bhopal Infantry were coming. The O.C. Royal Fusiliers, being the senior officer in the vicinity, asked that the battalion take up a defensive position where they stood and dig in. On conferring with the O.C. S.Lancs, Maj. Roche persuaded the O.C. Royal Fusiliers that better fire positions could be obtained by moving back At 9p.m. the move was made, with the 1/Wilts going back some 500/600 yards.

The actions between 23rd-27th October had caused casualties of 14 officers and 350 Other Ranks. The Germans took seven of the officers as prisoners, a sure sign that the battalion had been in a desperate position. The War Diary for 27th contains two witness statements accounting for the action, suggesting

---

13 *At this time Pte. Tanner was being executed - but clearly the 1/Wilts had other things on their mind that day.*

14 *A vivid account of the 2/Royal Irish Rifles' actions during 1914 is given in J. F. Lucy's 'There's a Devil in the Drum'.*

15 *The timings given in the War Diary are confusing.*

16 *Units from the Indian Army, having arrived via Marseilles, were now in the area.*

that the loss of Neuve Chapelle was not a thing to be dismissed lightly either by the battalion or by its higher command.

On 28th 2 companies of Sappers and Miners relieved the 1/Wilts position in the small hours of the morning. The men were taken back to Pont Logy.[17] After a brief rest they were warned for an attack on Neuve Chapelle, but they were not required. Then the battalion marched off to billets at Richebourg St. Vaast, marching in at 10a.m. with 5 officers and 200 men. Here they found a party of reinforcements. The casualty rate the previous day had been high - around 150 men killed or wounded, and a further 150 missing believed prisoners. Just a few hours later they were ordered back to Pont Logy to assist the 2nd Cavalry Brigade. After a comfortless night bivouacked in a field the 1/Wilts moved out of the line back to La Couture - their day being cheered by receiving a "large consignment of mail, warm clothing, and gifts from friends at home". There followed a period of rest at Locre[18], reached via Doulieu and Nord Helf (a mile north of Merris). They were now back in Belgium and in the vicinity of Ypres.

---

17 *Pt. Logis on modern maps.*

18 *Loker on modern maps.*

Chapter 2 - 1914-1915 - Stalemate

The First Winter

At Locre they met up with a brother officer of the 2/Wilts, who would have been able to give an account of that battalion's doings since arriving with the 7th Division - including details of their action on 24th October, when they had been reduced to 250 men. On 4th November it was noted that the 1/Wilts had lost 26 officers and 1000 men since arriving in France - the equivalent of a whole battalion. This represents an average daily casualty rate of about 12 since the battalion landed in France.

Then, on 5th November, the battalion moved to Hooge via Ypres, and were in the front line or reserve trenches for the next 16 days. The *Official History* records that there was a reorganisation of forces at this point into 7 groups, and Br.Gen. McCracken's force (2/S. Lancs, 1/Wilts, 1/Gordon Highlanders, 2/R. Irish Rifles) was put in the line between the left of Cavan's group and the Menin[1] Road, and to the right of Br. Gen. Count Gleichen's group. The War Diary records the daily attrition through shelling and the appalling conditions in the trenches. There were alarms and counter-attacks repulsing Germans who infiltrated parts of the line. Elsewhere the battle was raging along the line from the English Channel, with Belgian, French as well as British and Empire troops involved. In the middle of November (17th) Maj. Roche was killed by shellfire, on the same day that Germans occupied 'D' Company's advanced trenches, necessitating their later ejection at bayonet point.

On 21st November the battalion moved out of the line to Westoutre for 'rest and reorganisation'. Five days later they were inspected and complemented upon by Sir John French. At the end of the month (30th) the 1/Wilts went back into the trenches in front of Kemmel, and for the rest of 1914 and right up until 22nd March 1915 the pattern of Locre (rest) and Kemmel (trenches) repeated itself. On 7th December Lt. Col. Hasted returned to resume command of the battalion. Christmas day was not one of football matches and fraternising with the enemy in no-man's-land. It was a fairly routine day with several casualties reported.

At the end of January 1915 the diarist makes a number of interesting observations regarding trench life:

---

1 *Menen on modern maps.*

Notes on the Operations during the past month.

The weather on the whole has been bad, and the conditions of the trenches has at times been of the worst. Towards the latter end of the month owing to better weather conditions, and also to the better supply of material, and the experience gained, the condition of the trenches has been much improved. The attached sketch [separate pencil drawing in handwritten book] shows roughly the type of trench used, but, trenches vary with the condition of the ground and the material which is available. Pumps have been found of the greatest value for keeping the water in the trenches under control. Sump pits at intervals in the floor have been left for boiling purposes. Some trenches have to be built almost entirely of sandbags. Communication trenches almost invariably get full of water, and for the most part are not practicable. The trenches are provided with a few loop holes at intervals for look out men and snipers. When not in use these are blinded. Loop holed iron plates are used to a certain extent, but are difficult to conceal and afford a mark for the enemy.
The system of relief is 4 days in the front line, and 4 days rest in billets about 3/4 miles in rear of the front line. When in the front line as far as possible (?) that actually front firing line trenches are relieved every night - it is found that a longer period causes the sickness to go up very rapidly. When resting every effort is made to keep the men fit, and to rest them: hot baths are supplied and if possible clean washing for every man, short route marches, fatigues work, classes of instruction etc. are carried out. There have been no actual active operations, the fighting being confined to intermittent shelling of our trenches, hardly a day passing without some shelling and artillery duels. As regards Infantry there has been continued sniping, mostly by night and not so heavy by day, occasional more by nervousness than anything else. The waste from battle casualties has been 18 killed and 16 wounded.

On 22nd February two N.C.O.s were commissioned, one being Cpl. Ogilvie who was to become such an important figure in the battalion's history during the war.

Spanbroek Molen and Hooge

In March 1915 the major area of operations centred on Neuve Chapelle. In order to support the attack at this place and prevent the Germans from withdrawing troops from elsewhere to bolster the defences, an attack on

Spanbroek Molen was ordered. The proposed objective was a German strongpoint just over a mile north of Wulverghem, and some 13 miles north of Neuve Chapelle. On 12th March 1915 at 2.45a.m. the 1/Wilts left Locre and marched via Kemmel to the trenches in front of Spanbroek Molen. They were in position by 5.30a.m., and there they waited for the artillery bombardment to begin. Due to mist this did not take place until 2.30p.m. on that day. The bombardment lasted for around 1½ hours, and consisted of shrapnel against the wire and high explosives to damage the trenches. The infantry assault by the 3/Worcs and 1/Wilts started at 4.10 p.m. (some 13½ hours after leaving Locre). Their way over trenches was made through use of 'flying bridges' laid previously, but the artillery bombardment had not been effective. The enemy were able to bring heavy machine gun and rifle fire to bear on their attackers. By 5p.m. the assault had faltered, and men were beginning to crawl back. By 7p.m. the battalion withdrew, survivors being able to use the dusk as a cover to return to their positions. They then faced the return march back to Locre. Casualties had been 7 officers and 86 O.R.s[2], although the 3/Worcs had suffered even more. The following day's War Diary entry simply reads 'Rest' - it is to be hoped that this was the literal meaning and not a euphemism for more fatigues.

For the next 3 months the battalion was engaged upon routine trench duty just south of Ypres, with spells out of the line at Dikkebus or La Clytte. The War Diary records a round of trench reliefs, working parties and the trickle of casualties due mainly to shelling. On 24th April Lt. Col. Hasted left the 1/Wilts due to sickness. There were very few of his brother officers who had embarked with him in August 1914 still with the battalion to bid him farewell.

An account of a visit to the trenches at about this time by the Divisional Commander (Maj. Gen. Haldane) is given by his Aide de Camp (Billy Congreave):[3]

> 8th June (1915)
> The General and I have been up to Hooge.[4] We went up via Sanctuary and Zouave Woods, where we found Blake in a dug-out (he now commands the Wilts). Everything was fairly peaceful - they still shell Zouave Wood, but not Sanctuary. Blake took us up to the 'village', then to the stables. It was hard to make anything out as the General

---

2 *Other Ranks.*

3 *From Armageddon Road A V.C.'s Diary.*

4 *The 1/Wilts were positioned astride the Ypres-Menin Road.*

was in such a hurry, and the place is such a maze of works and debris that one needs a day up there to realise where one is and what is best to be done. Suddenly down came the rain. The heat had been awful and now we were soaked through. The trenches were a few inches deep in mud and water almost at once.

Bellewaarde

The routine was disturbed by attacks on the Germans later on in June. On 16th June (Congreave's diary, which gives an account, dates it the 17th June) an assault was made following a bombardment of an hour or so in the early hours of the morning. This would appear to have been successful, with 'C' and 'D' Companies effecting entry into the German trench system, progressing with the liberal use of bombs.[5] Around 6a.m. to 9 a.m. work was done on the captured trench network to improve the defensive position. By 10.30 a.m. the Germans had counter-attacked, by which time the supply of bombs had given out. The men were slowly forced back with numerous casualties. A further attack on the enemy was met with more casualties, and by mid-afternoon the artillery took over, with both sides heavily shelling each other. The toll was 9 officers and nearly 200 O.R.s killed, wounded, or missing. This action was part of a larger one aimed against the Bellewaarde ridge. The ridge was well placed for enemy observation, and represented a bulge into the allied lines. Careful preparations were made for the attack, including triplicate cabling for communications and patrolling by the R.F.C.[6] The men were given extra ammunition, and battalions were equipped with grenades and wire cutters. The line formed a right angle at Bellewaarde, running north-south, and at the southern point turning eastwards. The 1/Wilts occupied a position just at this turning point, facing northwards. The main attack was to be against the north-south line of enemy trenches, but the successive lines of assaulting troops got mixed up and confused. This caused the attack to loose its impetus. Meanwhile the 1/Wilts attacked, as described above, towards Hooge. Map 4 shows the area of operations on 16th June.

Six days later another attack was made. On 22nd June, following an half-hour bombardment, 2 platoons of 'A' Company went into the attack, but they were held up by machine gun fire. German positions were virtually intact following the bombardment. Billy Congreave's diary gives a bystander's account:

---

5 *i.e. grenades.*

6 *Royal Flying Corps.*

19 June 1915 The Wilts go up to take over Hooge tonight. Blake now commands the Wilts and does it well. I expect they will put Hooge to rights soon.

21 June…. later: It has been decided that the Wilts are to go at the redoubt tomorrow night, after dark. There is to be a half-hour bombardment first, also a simultaneous attack by the 14th Div. …. to my mind a half-hour bombardment by a few guns is just like giving a fellow notice that you are going to kick him…..

22 June The attack failed miserably.

23 June Apparently the shelling was not effective enough. The Wilts came under heavy fire as soon as they showed themselves. The Boche[7] was all warned and ready so naturally it failed.

Trench Routine 1915

For the next 6 months or thereabouts, the battalion carried on its pattern of static trench warfare in the Hooge area. The period was not without incident, and certainly not without casualties. The whole diary for this period is about shelling, fatigues repairing trenches, wiring, and the routine of trench life. For example, on 8th June the War Diary simply records: "Fine and thundery. Relieved by HAC.[8] 1 killed, 3 wounded." The man killed would appear to have been Acting Sgt. Ernest Smith who had previously been shot in May, the bullet striking his pocket watch, probably saving his life on that occasion. The watch was sent home as a souvenir, but arrived there just after notification of his death on the 8th.[9]

Enemy action was not the only danger facing soldiers: accidents were not uncommon, and in June the M.O.,[10] Lt. Pryn, was accidently burned and subsequently died from his injuries. Earlier, on the 12th, an accident with a Lyddite grenade killed 2/Lt. Stansfield-Smith. There were casualties from the enemy's trench mortars, and incursions to be repelled. A new C.O., Lt. Col.

---

7 *i.e. the Germans.*

8 *Honourable Artillery Company.*

9 *Details concerning Ernest Smith to be found on http://www.ejgreen.freeserve.co.uk/downton/war14smithe.htm. Cpl. Smith is commemorated on Panel 53, Menin Gate Memorial, Ypres.*

10 *Medical Officer.*

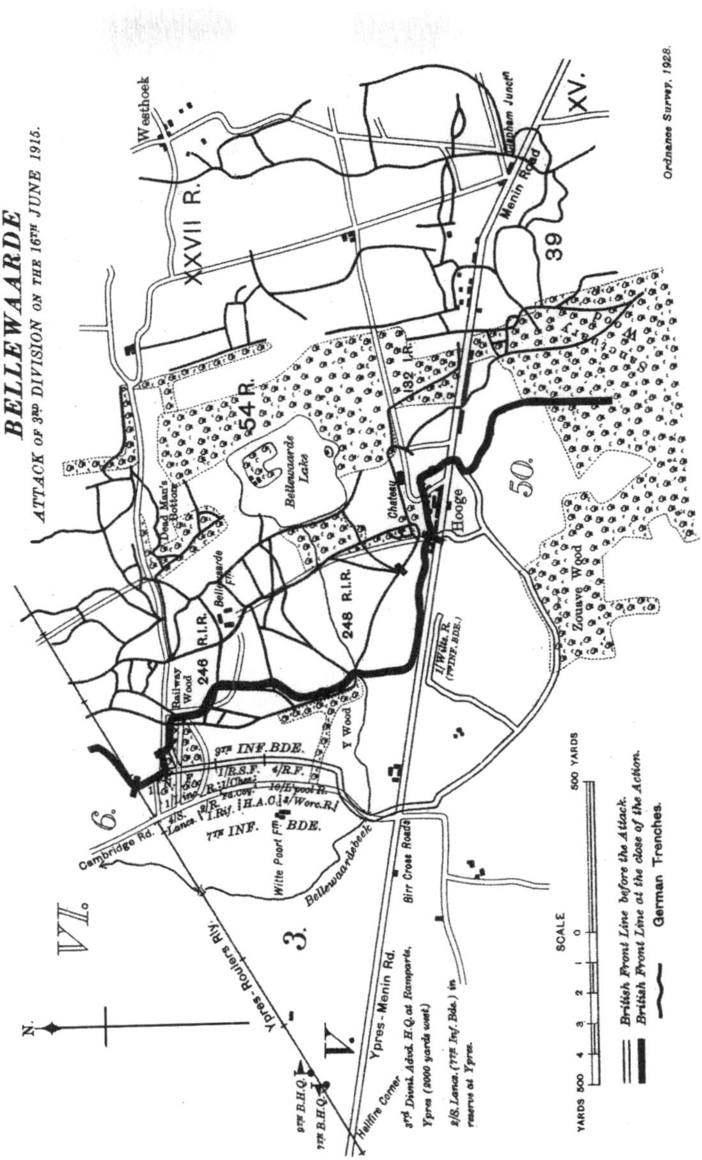
BELLEWAARDE
ATTACK OF 3RD DIVISION ON THE 16TH JUNE 1915.
Ordnance Survey, 1928.
Westhoek
XXVII R.
Menin Road
Clapham Junctn
XV.
39
54 R.
Bellewaarde Lake
Dead Man's Bottom
Chateau
132 I.R.
Hooge
50.
Zouave Wood
Railway Wood
246 R.I.R.
248 R.I.R.
Bellewaarde Fm.
Y Wood
1/Wilts.R. (7TH INF. BDE.)
9TH INF. BDE.
1/R.S.F.
4/R.F.
1/N.F.
1/Linc. R.
1/Ches.
10/L'pool R.
4/S. Lancs.
2/R.I.Rif.
H.A.C.
3/Worc.R.
7TH INF. BDE.
Cambridge Rd.
Witte Poort Fm.
Bellewaardbeek
Birr Cross Roads
Ypres-Roulers Rly.
Ypres-Menin Rd.
Hellfire Corner
9TH B.H.Q.
7TH B.H.Q.
3rd Divnl. Advd. H.Q. at Ramparts, Ypres (2000 yards west.)
2/S. Lancs. (7TH Inf. Bde.) in reserve at Ypres.
VI.
6.
3.
V.
N.
SCALE
YARDS 500
500 YARDS
British Front Line before the Attack.
British Front Line at the close of the Action.
German Trenches.

Map 4

Brown, arrived towards the end of July. They celebrated this event by exploding a mine near a crater on the front line. Later that month (29th and 30th July) the Germans demonstrated that they too could set off mines. The first one was 10 yards in front of the trenches, and minimal casualties were sustained. A further (and more devastating) mine exploded on 1st August, killing one and wounding a dozen more.

Senior officers continued to pay further visits to the front line. Later that month (26th) both the Corps and Divisional commanders also visited the battalion. Previously, on 16th August, the Brigadier-General had called by to see them.

The growing importance of 'bombing' is illustrated in the entry for 27th August, when the 1/Wilts were ordered to occupy and fortify an old advanced trench and link it up with work being carried out by the 2/S. Lancs. On that occasion a bombing duel ensued with the enemy, and the battalion's grenadiers used 500 bombs.

On 2nd September, just before the Battle of Loos, the Germans subjected the trenches occupied by the battalion to fierce counter-bombardment. This was evidently due to their suspecting the onset of an offensive. The following day brought an apologetic and congratulatory note from the Divisional Commander. Later in that month (25th September) another assault on the enemy trenches around Hooge took place, with 1/Wilts in support of the Royal Irish Rifles and 2/S. Lancs. The Germans promptly responded to the British bombardment, and the position in the line was made very uncomfortable. The attacks by the Royal Irish Rifles and South Lancs were repulsed, and the starting lines of these battalions were manned by the 1/Wilts. The diary entry is remarkable in that it gives a detailed list of recommendations and suggestions stemming from their experience during the action. These are worth repeating here:

Points of Interest

> 1. Value of assembly slits and new trenches dug overnight. B Coy suffered very few casualties in slits S of MENIN road, these trenches had apparently not been registered and were not under direct observation. The half of A Coy had only 1 casualty in the new trench dug during night to the rear of the existing one H12. The new trench was carefully concealed with turf and light head cover was constructed to afford protection from shrapnel and falling pieces of shell. This

trench was never apparently observed.
2. Telephonic Communication was of no value. It would seem to be essential to establish come simple form of visual signalling between fire trenches and nearest supports.
3. The functions of CTs[11] were registered points & were shelled during the day. This is not the most suitable place to post guards to direct movement up & down the trenches. Head cover should be erected for such posts. The majority of CT trench guards were killed.
4. The CTs though blown in may places were used throughout the day and were of the utmost value for evacuating wounded and relieving congestion in the front lines.
5. The importance of all ranks knowing position of Battn HQ, much delay and possibly many casualties were occasioned by orderlies bringing messages to the wrong headquarters.
6. There did not appear to be much advantage in having a dressing station in so advanced & exposed position. Only walking cases could be dealt with during the day & such could well have been attended to further back.
7. Artillery slits off the CTs were of value in drawing and distributing the enemy's fire. A large quantity of ammunition was expended in the slits off CASTLE ST in front of F2. These were unoccupied. Dummy trenches & barricades on the Wed might have been of considerable value in drawing the enemies fire from occupied trenches: if time had been available to construct them.

The casualty bill for this day's work was 2 officers and 68 O.R.s. More trench life with working parties then followed, with the occasional casualty, including a sergeant wounded by a premature shell exploding as it hit a tree branch shortly after firing. Doubtless the trips to the baths at Poperinghe would have offered a welcome opportunity to clean up.

11 *Communication Trench.*

Chapter 3 - With the 25th Division and on the Somme

In mid October (17th) the battalion (with the rest of 7th Brigade) parted company with 3rd Division, having been with them since the start of hostilities. Maj. Gen. Haldane made a farewell speech to the officers and men, and gave well-earned praise for their achievements in the line. He was rewarded with three cheers, after which he distributed medals. The battalion then marched to Bailleul, helped on its way by music (including 'Auld Lang Syne') by the divisional band. The unit was able to rest, reorganise and train until it resumed front line service by relieving the 8/Loyals at Ploegsteert Wood in 1st November. This battalion, with 10/Cheshire and 3/Worcs were with 1/Wilts as part of 7th Brigade in 25th Division.

The new division had been raised towards the end of 1914, seeing service around Ypres. 7th Brigade was a replacement for 76th Brigade, which left the division. This was the result of a policy then of ensuring that each 'Kitchener' division had one regular brigade in its components. Lt. A.J.S. White reported that:[1]

> The regular battalions, Wiltshires and Worcestershires, held the other (north country) battalions in great contempt, which was probably unjustified: by this stage of the war the regular battalions contained no more regular officers or men than did the Kitchener's army battalions.

The battalion stayed a full week in the trenches at Ploegsteert Wood. The change of air seemed to suit them, as they had notable successes at sniping. On 3rd November 2 of the enemy were shot, and the next day Lt. Russell was reported as doing good work with snipers. Even better results were obtained on 6th November, when 8 Germans were 'knocked over' by snipers. The enemy also had the inconvenience of having 6 periscopes and 2 sniper plates destroyed. These successes would have helped the men keep cheerful, as they were reported to be, even though the rain meant that trenches were collapsing.

The rest of 1915 was seen out either in the trenches at Ploegsteert Wood, or out of the line at Papot or 'The Piggeries' (one of the more apt names for the encampments springing up just behind the front line). Again, the ordinary trench routine is amply illustrated in the War Diary, with busy schedules out

---

1 *Recollections.*

of line on training and working parties. Reference is made on 27th December to a catapult device used for throwing 'bombs' - so unsuccessfully that it backfired and wounded 2 men, one severely. This was a not uncommon experience with these and some other new-fangled devices tried out in the front line.

The Ploegsteert Wood/Papot tour of duty continued up until 24th January 1916. New Year's Day was also celebrated as Christmas, with roast pork, beer etc. The weather was mild, and the 1/Wilts kept up their sniping habits. The wayward catapult device brought further trouble on the battalion's head on 5th January, when a retaliatory German artillery bombardment was blamed on the Wiltshires' catapult and mortars. Luckily little harm was done, with the men continuing sniping.

The stay at Outtersteene, starting on 24th January, was to be the longest settled stay for the battalion during the war years. The men were housed in barns attached to farms. A roll of N.C.O.s in each of the four companies is attached to the entry for 27th. This gives a strength of 140, with one being away at a divisional school. An analysis of the N.C.O. list is given at Appendix E. It shows the varied tasks and specialisms allotted. Intensive training and physical exercise marked the period out of line. On 9th February they were inspected by the Army Commander (Plumer) - his comments are not recorded. Three days later the Corps Commander visited and presented medal ribbons. A proposed visit by the Commander-in-Chief (Sir Douglas Haig) in early March had to be cancelled due to weather. This finally took place on 31st March at a field near Tincques, where the battalion was complemented upon for the way they moved their arms, and their fitness. (This had been well-honed over the previous few months through football, cross-country runs, route marches etc). From 10th March onwards the 1/Wilts moved in stages south towards the Arras area. Whilst at these staging camps - Valhoun, Ternas - training continued. On 3rd April a fire broke out in one of the barns being used, and the following day was taken up by an 'extensive enquiry' into the affair. Amidst so much destruction the accidental burning of a barn was not to be treated lightly!

At the Front again

Then, on 10th April, the battalion moved east to the Mont St. Eloi/La Targette area. Early in March the British had agreed to take on an additional 20 miles of the front line, from Ransart past Arras, Vimy, Souchez, and Lens, to Loos. Mont St. Eloi lies some 7.5km north west of Arras. La Targette some 4km east of Mont St. Eloi, the whole in the vicinity of Vimy Ridge. During their time on this sector of the front there was hectic mining, and sniping activity by both sides. The Germans had made a head start in the mining business, and the R.E. Tunnelling Companies had yet to win dominance in the war underground. One of the problems with mines was that of capturing and holding the crater made. An alert enemy, if they overcame the shock promptly, stood a better chance of capturing the crater than the side doing the mining since, naturally, they were nearer and did not have to cross a contested no man's land. The 1/Wilts spent some time on 21st/22nd April in practising crater consolidation. In this sector both British and French mining companies were at work, as were the Germans. The battalion played an active part in all this, fetching and carrying, and actually working in the tunnels. During late April early May the Germans seem to have had the edge over the British, although this particular form of warfare seems to have been denied them after 9th May. Fig. 1 below illustrates the numbers.

Date	Allied Mines	German Mines
16th April	2 (French)	
17th April		1
18th April		1
24th April		1
3rd May		2
4th May		1
8th May	1	1
9th May		1

Fig. 1. Mines blown 16th April - 9th May, 1915.

This regular blowing of mines was accompanied by sniping and trench mortar exchanges, and duels with the enemy over craters and trenches. The Brigade Major of the 7th Brigade at this time was Alexander Johnston of the Worcestershire Regt. His diary[2] at this time adds detail to the 1/Wilts War Diary account.

> 24th April 1916… At 7.30 p.m. the earth shook like an earthquake, the dug-outs quivered, and of course we knew that a mine had gone up…….and very soon after the mine went up, the Huns started a bomb

2 *Extracts may also be found in 'Arras Vimy Ridge' (Battleground Europe series) by Nigel Cave.*

attack against the1st Wilts from Grange Crater: the1st Wilts stopped that all right but had 2 officers wounded and another killed in trying to get across and get in touch with 10/Cheshires.
3rd May 1916 ...we were kept busy by the Huns blowing this time two mines under or near our front line: there was five seconds between them, one was under a bit of our front line but only got 3 of our men, and the other was about 30 yards in front of our line. The Germans were quickly out but the old 1st Wilts were quite equal to the occasion, turned a machine gun on to the Germans as they came forward, and then rushed up and started digging on the near lip covered by bombers who kept the enemy bombers back without difficulty........ Also went up to both the new craters where 1/Wilts had got on in great style: there was a good deal of bombing going on, and when I had a look into one of the craters one of the Wilts bombers at my side was hit but not badly, I am glad to say.
4th May 1915 ... Yet another mine up in the evening, again on the1st Wilts front, and again they had the situation well in hand, and consolidated on the near lip of the crater.

8th May was a particularly hectic. There was rifle-grenading from the German side of Common Crater, and an enemy sniper killed a valued officer, Lt. E. E. Brown. The War Diary gives a brief résumé of his exploits with the battalion. At 7.57 p.m. a mine went up between two existing craters at the top of Birkin C.T. This caused casualties, and required consolidation, but otherwise left a topography more favourable to the British. Sixteen minutes later the British sprang a mine at the top of Grange C.T. This formed a long and deep crescent shaped crater that required consolidation and action to hinder German work. On the 9th the new Brigadier-General (Heathcote) was shown around the trenches.[3] The Germans welcomed him with another mine, blown at 7.46p.m. (this appears to be a favoured time of the day for this sort of activity) north of Albany C.T. crater. This was not unexpected and the area had been evacuated. Alexander Johnston noted in his diary that the 1/Wilts "were soon on the near lip consolidating, and had the situation well in hand at once, though there was some fairly heavy bombing for a bit." The battalion had evidently learned the lessons from its April crater consolidation exercise. On 18th May Broadmarsh crater was lost to the Germans by the 10/Cheshires, to the north of the 1/Wilts position. The 1/Wilts reported the enemy's attitude as being 'quiet', although Johnston's diary tells of attempts by 10/Cheshires

3 *Johnston seemed to have spent a lot of time accompanying the General around the trenches - this General (along with others) did not skulk away in the safety of a rear-based chateau!*

to re-capture the crater at first through an exchange of bombs, but later with rifle and bayonet. As an aside, it is interesting to note that it took Johnston's personal intervention to get the men to use rifles instead of bombs. This over-reliance on bombs was a cause for concern with senior commanders.

On the day following the loss of the Broadmarsh crater fresh assaults were made by 8/Loyals and 10/Cheshires. This brought on firing along the whole of that sector, and 1/Wilts had to take their share. With the recapture of Broadmarsh, 1/Wilts loaned some Lewis guns to assist their comrades in the anticipated counter-attack. On 21st May the Germans launched a determined attack in this part of the front, preceded by a bombardment including gas and lachrymatory shells. Their attacks made inroads into the British position, and attempts to oust the Germans only succeeded in part. The *Official History* notes that a British deserter gave the plan away, and German artillery fire and confusion on the British side prevented the attack from meeting all its objectives. The position had to be accepted since plans for the Somme offensive were now well advanced, and resources could not be diverted. This sector had to wait until 1917 for redress. Map 5 shows the area of operations in May.

The 1/Wilts stayed in this area, in the Pylones trenches, until 1st June. During this time the War Diary paints a vivid picture of constant work and fighting, with a steady flow of casualties. This spell also marked the longest continuous period of duty in the trenches, some 21 days.

At the beginning of June the battalion moved westwards to Chelers. A gap appears in the War Diary, but Kincaid-Smith's [4] book tells us that the Division were in training west of St. Pol. A fortnight later they moved south to Barly via Penin then, after a few days to Gézaincourt, Halloy lès Pernois, Puchevillers and finally to Varennes - drawing ever closer to the Somme battlefield.

The Somme

The time and place for a 'push' in 1916 was determined to a large extent by the German attack on the French at Verdun. Verdun was to be a battle of attrition, and the French were sorely pressed on this front. The fresh divisions raised by Kitchener were beginning to assemble in the B.E.F. area in large numbers. Part of the aim for the offensive would therefore be to relieve the pressure on

---

4 *'The 25th Division in France and Flanders'.*

VIMY RIDGE
21ST MAY 1916.

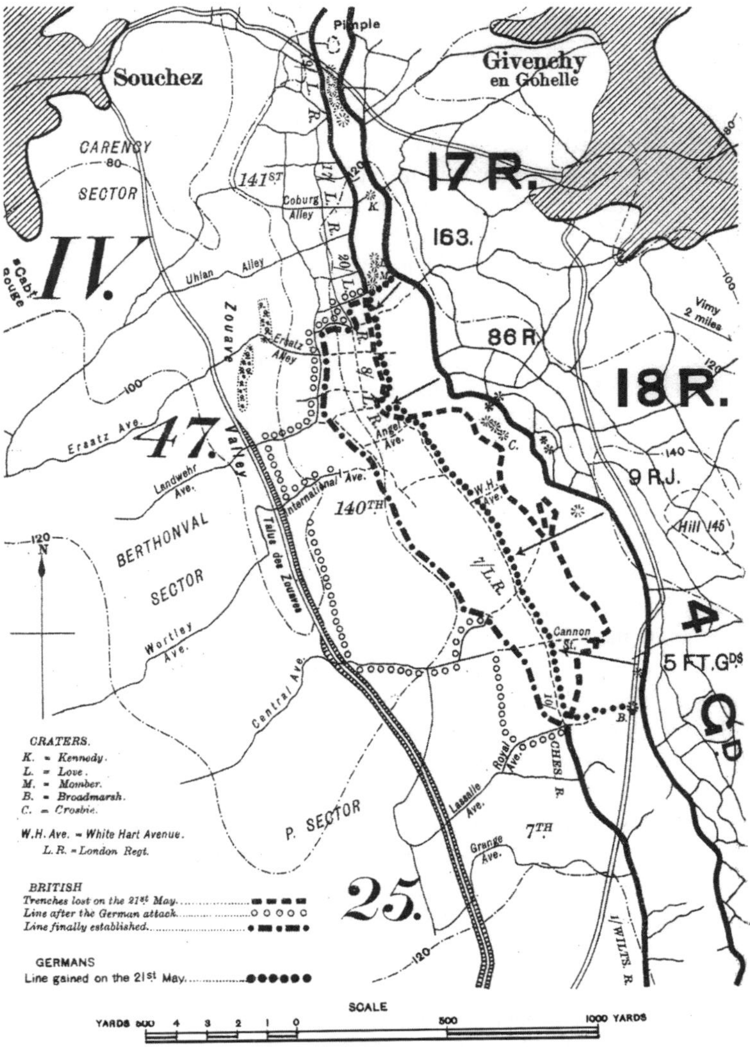

Map 5

the French by giving the Germans something else to think about. The area for the offensive was to extend something like 8 miles either side of the Bapaume-Albert road on the north bank of the Somme. The French were to attack south of the British lines in the area of the Somme and immediately south of the river.

The 1st July 1916 marked the opening of the battle, and the appalling casualties associated with that first day. The 1/Wilts were fortunate to be spared that experience, and spent the day resting for their coming part in the campaign. On 2nd orders were given to move forward, although the 'B' team stayed with Divisional transport. By this time the commanders were concerned by the losses that were being incurred through attacks, and a cadre of officers and men were selected (the 'B' team) to stay back and form the nucleus of a reformed battalion if casualties proved excessive. They could also be used as an emergency reserve. On 3rd July the battalion took over trenches captured from the enemy on 1st July, in the vicinity of Leipzig Salient. This heavily defended feature stuck out from the German line, on a spur, just south of Thiepval and on the north side of Nab Valley. Map 6 indicates the area of operations around Thiepval.

On 5th July the 1/Wilts made their first attack in this battle, and the enemy's second line was given as the objective. This was originally to be on a front of 600 yards, but was later changed to 300 yards[5]. The formation to be employed is described in the War Diary: 'C' Company (Capt. G. B. Russell) on the right and 'D' Company (Capt. R. L. Knubley) on the left. Each would have 3 platoons up front and 1 platoon in support. 'B' Company would act as support and provide carrying parties. A 6p.m. start was later changed to 7p.m., and this was preceded by a half-minute artillery bombardment assisted by Stokes mortars. Once over the top the men were met with fierce rifle and machine gun fire. 'C' Company made their objectives with few casualties, but 'D' Company were badly cut up, and the numbers reaching their objective were insufficient to contain the enemy's immediate counter-attack. This ejection was temporary as supporting platoons were able to regain the initiative. There followed an intense artillery bombardment by the enemy, and this resulted in the loss of the C.O., Lt. Col. W. S. Brown, and the wounding of R.S.M. Parker and others. Capt. Ogilvie, commissioned from the ranks some 17 months before, assumed command of the battalion for the first time. As a result of the day's action 20 were killed in action, 158 wounded, and a further 22 missing. A heavy bill, yet not as bad as that experienced by many units on the first day. The War Diary for the day ends with recommendations for awards.

5 *Kincaid-Smith's book gives a 500 yard front attacked.*

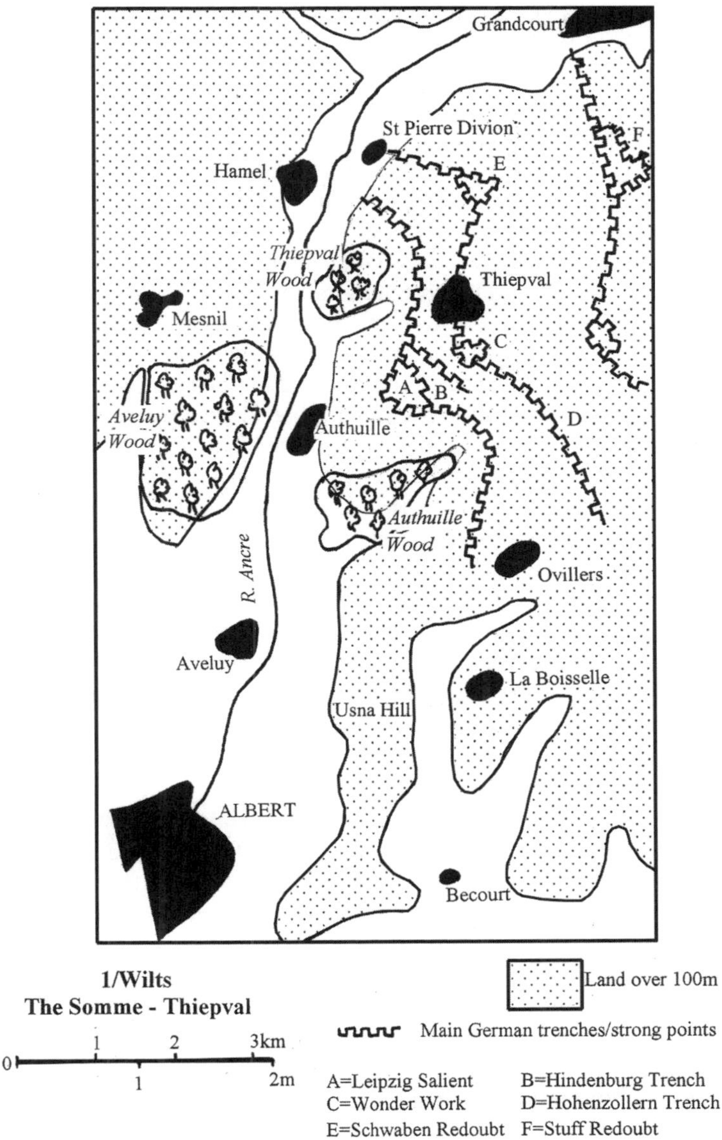
Grandcourt
St Pierre Divion
F
E
Hamel
Thiepval Wood
Thiepval
Mesnil
C
A
B
Aveluy Wood
Authuille
D
Authuille Wood
Ovillers
R. Ancre
Aveluy
La Boisselle
Usna Hill
ALBERT
Becourt
1/Wilts
The Somme - Thiepval
0 1 2 3km
1 2m
Land over 100m
Main German trenches/strong points
A=Leipzig Salient
B=Hindenburg Trench
C=Wonder Work
D=Hohenzollern Trench
E=Schwaben Redoubt
F=Stuff Redoubt

Map 6

Further assaults on Leipzig Salient were to be made against their objective of two days earlier. Whilst a conference was taking place to discuss details of the proposed attack, the enemy launched a counter-attack at 1.15a.m. on the trench captured by 'C' Company. Lt. R. J. A. Palmer and his men beat off this effort, but fierce bombing continued through the remainder of the night. None of this seems to have deterred the plans for an attack, and at 9.30a.m. (after a brief but intensive bombardment by guns and Stokes mortars) 2 waves of 3 platoons each attacked the enemy trench. The attack was expected, and the enemy put up a fierce resistance. Battalion snipers were lodged in shell holes in front of the line and used steel nosed bullets to knock out machine guns. This proved effective, but there were still heavy casualties. Their efforts were crowned with success but the captured trench was wide, and therefore offered less protection from the enemy artillery, which then turned itself on the position. Sergeant J. Hillings earned a bar to his D.C.M. that day, the citation reading:

> On the 7th July, 1916, at the Leipzig Salient during the capture of an enemy trench, this N.C.O. displayed the finest qualities of bravery and coolness under intense shell fire. This N.C.O. was Acting Company Sergeant Major. His company commander and company officers were killed very early, and he took command of the company. Under very heavy shell fire he encouraged his men, supervised the erection of blocks and the general consolidation of the trench with such marked ability that it was held in spite of frequent attempts on the part of the enemy to bomb the company out of it.

Their opponents during this engagement included, according to the *Official History*, the *Guard Fusiliers (3rd Guard Div.).* That evening the battalion was relieved and went to nearby Crucifix Corner to rest. Kincaid-Smith records the casualties for 1/Wilts over the past few days as 26 officers and 400 men killed and wounded. On the following day Capt. Ogilvie was required to go over to Usna Hill to view the situation at the front. Later that evening the battalion moved on to Usna Hill, which was to be their home for the next 5 days. Special Divisional orders on that day recorded the part played by both the 1/Wilts and 3/Worcs in action over the previous days. The fighting strength of the battalion was put at around 200 men.

The battalion moved out of the battle area until 23rd July, during which period the War Diary records them as resting, re-fitting, taking in fresh drafts, and training. On 23rd they occupied trenches at Hamel, on the west bank of the River Ancre. This was routine trench duty, and ended 6 days later. A longish spell out of the line followed with training and, on 12th August, lining the road at Sarton to cheer King George V.

On 18th August it was back into the trenches at Leipzig Salient. An attack was made on the enemy's position on 22nd August[6] in conjunction with the 4/Gloucesters and this resulted in the capture of a section of trenches. As usual, heavy retaliatory bombardments followed. Casualties were put at 90. Cpl. Vine won the D.C.M. as one of the first into the enemy trench, where he "did great execution with his rifle and bayonet." Cpl. Vine was then wounded three times whilst helping in consolidating the trench. On the previous night he had carried out a solitary patrol of the enemy wire in full moonlight. Other men were also put forward for awards. This action was remarkable, according to Kincaid-Smith, for being the first occasion the Division had used a 'push pipe mine'.[7] A further assault on the enemy's lines was mounted on 24th[8] along with the 3/Worcesters. At 4.10 p.m. an artillery barrage was started, and under its cover the attacking forces went over. Three companies - 'A' (2/Lt. W.J. Ross), 'B' (Capt. B.S. Mackin) and 'D' (Capt L.H.Horncastle) led the attack with 'C' Company (Capt. G.D. Brown) in support. At 4.12 p.m. two 'push mines' were exploded to provide cover. Except for the extreme left, objectives (the Hindenburg trench) were reached and consolidated. The War Diary lists the reference numbers of the trenches involved. Kincaid-Smith attributes the success in part to the surprise factor, the effectiveness of the creeping barrage, and a diversionary smoke barrage near Thiepval Wood which drew the enemy's fire. Casualties during the actual assault were light, although the retaliatory shellfire took its toll - trenches taken had been badly knocked about and provided little protection from such fire. Some accounts (but not the War Diary or Kincaid Smith) relate that the *Prussian Guard* - regarded as an elite unit - attempted to retake the positions but were repulsed. On 26th the battalion was relieved and came out of the line. Their efforts, along with those of other units, had nibbled away at the German strongpoint at Leipzig Salient.

A further period of rest, training and refitting followed. It is disappointing to read that the official photographer, who visited on 29th at Bouzincourt, was

---

6 *Kincaid-Smith puts it as being on 21st. The recommendations for awards given in the War Diary give 23rd!*

7 *This was a machine used in civil engineering to bore horizontal holes through which pipes could run - or explosives. When blown the explosives would create a 'trench'.*

8 *Kincaid-Smith seems to put this attack as having taken place on 25th September.*

1/Wilts attacking on the Somme.

unable to take any pictures due to the dull and wet weather. Then, on 3rd September, it was back to the trenches at Leipzig Salient. The troops were to move up to the trenches during the night, and take a series of trenches. Following a bombardment of the enemy positions the attack went in, only to be met by heavy enemy 'whizbang' and machine gun fire. The attack failed with heavy casualties, and the survivors were order out of the line again that evening. For the rest of the month (until 30th September) the battalion moved around various locations behind the line.

It was then back to the trenches at Thiepval (which had been captured on 27th September) and vicinity. These trenches - Hessian, Stuff Redoubt and Zollern - were just to the north east of Thiepval. Normal trench duties were followed whilst in the front line. Towards the end of October (23rd) they moved out of the Somme battlefield area progressing to Gézaincourt (on the outskirts of Doullens).

Gen. Sir Hubert Gough, 5th Army, sent the 25th Division the following message[9] as they left his command:

> It is with great regret that the Commander of the Reserve Army bids farewell to Maj.- Gen. Bainbridge and the 25th Division. This Division has the proud distinction of having served longer in the Somme battle than any other in the Army. During the past four months it has been successful in many engagements, had taken many prisoners and has inflicted very heavy losses upon the enemy. These successes are due to good leadership and sound organisation in the higher ranks and to a spirit of cheerfulness, courage and resolution in the junior ranks, officers and men. It has every reason to be proud of these achievements and this spirit.

On 26th October the Commander-in-Chief inspected them. This made quite an impression on the newly arrived 2/Lt. A. J. S. White:[10]

> We marched back 20 miles or so to Gézaincourt and spent five days there, during which, in view of the way the regiment had recently covered itself with glory, the Commander-in-Chief, Sir Douglas Haig decided to inspect us. We lined the main street of the village and I was horrified to find that a man in my platoon just behind me was drunk

---

9 *Quoted in Kincaid-Smith's 'The 25th Division in France and Flanders'.*

10 *Recollections.*

> and was being propped up by the man on either side. He was beginning to cause trouble and I had to decide whether to remove him or hope for the best. He was taken off struggling, unfortunately just as the C-in-C came round the corner. But I shall not forget the sight of a very handsome man riding into the village with his escort of a squadron of Lancers behind him. He singled me out to speak to first, which was strange for no one could have looked less like a battered veteran: but when I confessed that I had arrived only 3 weeks before, he said - "Well you are very fortunate to join such a fine battalion."

At the end of the month (29th) they moved on to Papot, and took over duty in the Ploegsteert sector just north of Armentieres.

Chapter 4 From the Somme to Messines

Ploegsteert

This sector of the front had experienced little change since the fighting of 1914, and the battalion settled down to normal trench routine - working parties repairing and strengthening their positions, coping with the deteriorating weather and, when out of line, training. This would have been familiar territory for those who had been with the battalion at end of 1915. Patrols, sniping and exchanges of artillery fire all took place. The Diary lists the duties, the incidents and the casualties, including that of 2/Lt. Awdrey on 22nd November. Lt. Awdrey had the misfortune to shoot himself whilst cleaning his revolver. The officer casualty list tactfully records him as having been wounded in action. Lt. A.J.S. White also describes the routine in *Recollections*:

> We now settled down in these parts to a routine which lasted throughout the winter. Each battalion would spend six days in the front line trenches, then six days in support (still in the trenches), then six days again in the front line and at last six days in Pont-de-Nieppe where we were in billets and one actually got into a bed at night. These six days were slightly marred by having to go up to the front line nearly every day to help with the maintenance of the trenches under the supervision of R.E. officers.

The War Diary substantially confirms the general pattern, although variations occur. At other points during the war 4 or 5 day rotations were practised. Fig. 2 below shows the movement of the battalion from 30th October 1916 to 16th January 1917. The sequence was followed by a fortnight's training at De Seule.

Location	Sequence of Days spent in location														
Papot	2									2					
Pont de Nieppe		12			6						3				3
Le Bizet			6				6		2				6		
Le Touquet				6		6						6			
The Trenches								6						7	

Fig. 2. Pattern of Trench/Reserve/Rest periods Winter 1916/17

Lt. White continues, giving a description of the trenches in these parts:

> On the way up to the line there was a gum-boot store where we drew high rubber waders reaching to our thighs, which we wore all the time in the trenches.....My first impression of the front line was of the peace that seemed to reign over the place, especially compared with the Somme battlefield, of the depth of the front line trenches... and of the mud. From now on, except for some help from duck-boards, we stood most of the time in mud....... The place was infested with rats.... To add to the squalor of our surroundings there was the smell of rotting corpses which it had been impossible to bury properly in this sort of ground.

Time out of the line offered a welcome respite since, as Lt. White notes:

> It was possible on days when we were out at rest and not having to go up to the line to work, to visit Bailleul a fairly big town six miles away where the H.Q. of our 25th Division was situated. Incidentally the G.O.C. of the Division was called "Butcher Bainbridge" because of his alleged propensity for volunteering his division for any desperate fighting. Bailleul was not a very lively town but at least it had an "Officers Club" and one felt one was back in civilisation. We used to hitch-hike there, not on cars for they were rarely seen, but on lorries. I attended an Old Marlburian [1] Dinner in Bailleul. "Butcher Bainbridge" was in the chair. I was sorry to find that such an unpopular man was an Old Marlburian.

At the end of the year (30th December, 1916) two Germans entered the trenches, and on being challenged, one was shot and the other escaped. The next day a board appeared over the German trenches enquiring as to the location of the dead German's grave. This was ignored.

Trench routine continued into the new year (1917). A suspected outbreak of measles occurred on 4th January, but on the following day this was proved incorrect, and a good bath and the disinfecting of clothes and blankets prescribed. On the 10th a brisk bombardment by artillery and Stokes mortars took place, with feeble response by the enemy. It was noticed that the Germans had taken to throwing bombs at their own barbed wire, the conclusion being that these were new drafts practising bomb throwing. A

---

1 *Several 1/Wilts officers had been educated at Marlborough College.*

week later (17th) the brigade moved to De Seule for a fortnight's training. An insight into battle tactics is given in the War Diary entry for 25th January. The men practised the capture of two objectives, a front line with its immediate support trenches and a second line. Specialists were given special duties: the snipers to rush out just previous to the assault and fire upon enemy machine guns and snipers, the bombers to push on down CTs and establish blocks, the signallers to establish telephone communication with the position when captured etc. The men were in fighting order and carried tools for the consolidation of the objective.

Then back to the front initially in support, then taking over a section of the line. The battalion prepared for an attack by practising on land where flags were used to mark the layout of enemy trenches. The attack came on 17th February, and was carried out in conjunction with the 10/Cheshires. The trenches were gained but not, seemingly, Factory Farm, a German strong point. Lt. Wait wrote home[2] "I expect you will have seen in the paper that a daylight raid was made on the 17th. Well that was 'C' Coy et moi! It was a great success. I have been promised leave as soon as leave opens again which will be soon, I expect." On 24th the battalion with the rest of the Division were withdrawn - in the case of 1/Wilts to Mont des Chats.[3] Training continued, but 2 days later mention is made of the reorganisation of the battalion. Hitherto the company had been the main tactical unit in battle. Henceforth it was to be the platoon - G.H.Q. letter O B 1919 was given as the authority for this. The diary expands:

> By this the Battn Bombing Section was broken up and each platoon became a separate fighting unit consisting of all arms, and made up of four sections, a Lewis Gun Section, a Bombing Section and two Riflemen Sections.

As if to emphasise this change, platoon football matches were held the following day! After training in various locations in the Hazebrouck-Bailleul area the battalion took over responsibility for a section of trenches in the Le Touquet sector, on the River Lys, on 5th April 1917. From then until the end of April there are many gaps in the War Diary. On 21st April, according to Kinciad-Smith, the 25th Division was transferred to the 2nd Anzac Corps, relieving the New Zealand Division a week later at Wulverghem. At the end

---

2 *Letter to Mother, 19th February, 1917.*

3 *Kincaid-Smith has them in the neighbourhood of St. Omer.*

'C' Company officers outside a dugout (undated).

of April another move into training areas around St Omer was made. On 7th May, for example, we discover the 1/Wilts practising new tactics:

> The mornings work included bayonet fighting, the training of bombing and rifle bombing Sections, the practise of the Attack at first by platoons, then by Coys, introducing movements in "snake" formation and extended order, great attention being paid to the parts played by the different Sections, Lewis gunners, Rifle bombers etc. The training of Signallers was carried out independently throughout the week, particular attention being given to instruction in "visual".

It is worth noting that despite of all the work done to bury telephone cables, battlefield conditions still led commanders to place reliance on visual signalling and runners. Otherwise the officers and men were continuing to work on refinements to the tactics introduced earlier in the year. This round of training was completed on 20th May, with the battalion moving to the Wulverghem area. Here they occupied themselves in patrols, working parties and other routine activities. Inevitably casualties were incurred during this time.

Messines 1917

The high ground south of Ypres, including the Messines Ridge, was a sore trial to the British, permitting observation over a wide area, and in particular the Ypres salient itself. Plans for its capture were postponed during 1916 in deference to the Somme offensive. However, the series of deep mines dug during 1915/16 were still intact, and ready to assist the assault now planned. The 1/Wilts therefore found themselves again occupying territory familiar from its spell of duty in March 1915. Map 7 refers.

On 6th June, whilst at Ravelsburg Hill on the outskirts of Bailleul, the battalion was notified of the forthcoming attack on Messines. The 25th Division was to attack the front from the Wulverghem-Messines road to the Wulverghem-Wytschaete road - just under ¾mile in length. At this point the front line ran approximately east-west. The Division was supported on its right by the New Zealanders, and on the left by 36th Division. The plan was for a series of mines to be fired at 3.10a.m. on the 7th June, the ones

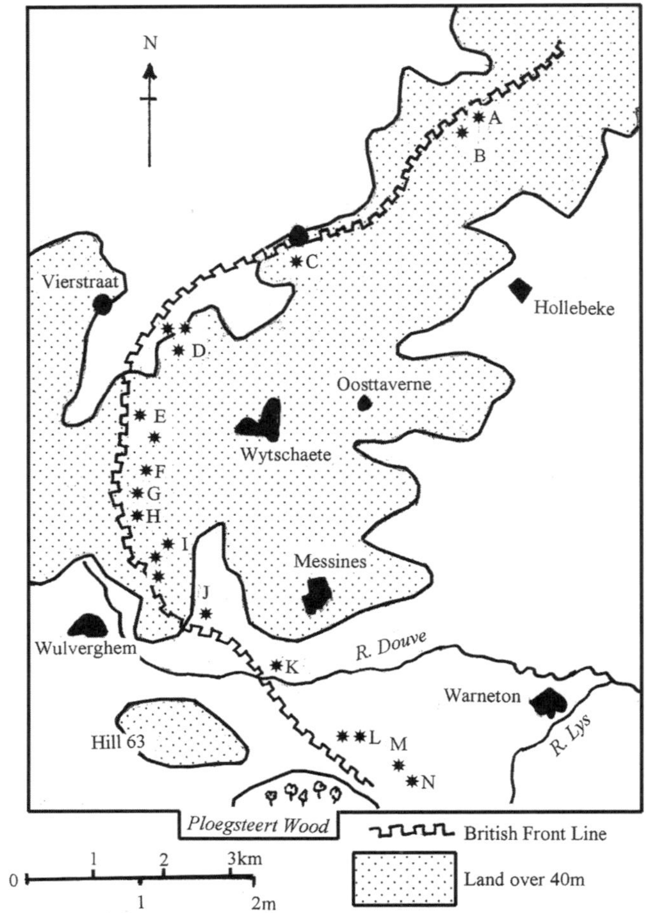

Mines (✱)

A - Hill 60	B - Caterpiller
C - St. Eloi	D - Hollandscheschuur Fm
E - Petit Bois	F - Maedelstede Farm
G - Peckham	H - Spanbroekmolen
I - Kruisstraat	J - Ontario Farm
K - Petit Douve Fm	L - Trench 127
M - Trench 122	N - Birdcage

1/Wilts
Messines 1917

Map 7

immediately on 25th Division's front being Ontario Farm[4] and Krusstraat.[5] This was to be the signal for an artillery bombardment of the enemy positions and for a series of leap-frogging infantry advances, capturing successive lines of German trenches. As they were captured they were to be consolidated, so as to ensure that a stout defence could be made in the event of a counter-attack.

The 1/Wilts assembled in specially prepared trenches prior to the mines being set off. They were not in the first wave of the assault, but moved off at 3.40a.m., in artillery formation[6], crossing the Steenbecque stream. 100 minutes later the battalion passed through the leading troops and achieved its first objective - October Trench. On the way they encountered a German concrete bunker with machine gun. This was dealt with and the machine gun used against the enemy. A hiccup now occurred, as the supporting artillery barrage did not lift in time, causing both delay and casualties through friendly fire. This, however, was a temporary set-back, the battalion going on to secure Four Huns Farm. At this point a gap developed between the 1/Wilts and the battalion of 36th Division immediately to their left. A machine gun at Lumm's Farm was able to exploit this, and Major Ogilvie collected a company of the Wilts and some assorted groups from other units and captured the position. The enemy garrison of 40 were either killed or captured. Further enemy positions were also eliminated before the battalion settled down to consolidating their position. At the end of the morning the 75th Brigade passed through the 1/Wilts, who spent time digging a new trench in front of October Trench (that position being so badly damaged by shellfire as to make consolidation impractical). This work continued on 8th June, with wire also being erected.

From 9th June until the night of 11th/12th June the 1/Wilts took over a section of the front line from 52nd Bttn Australian Imperial Forces. The line was called Odious Trench, and the relief was effected at night and with some difficulty owing to Australian guides losing their way. After this spell in the trenches the battalion drew back and took stock. During the period 7th-11th the 1/Wilts had captured 148 prisoners and 7 machine guns for the loss of 3 officers killed (1 died of wounds later) and 26 men, 2 officers and 96 men

4 *Completed 6/6/17, with a depth of 104 ft. containing 60,000lbs of ammonal*

5 *A total of 4 mines in this vicinity, dug between 50-60ft in depth each containing around 30,000 lbs of ammonal with additional guncotton.*

6 *In essence this meant in diagonal 'Indian File'. Used to reduce casualties from artillery fire.*

wounded. Up to the 20th June the battalion was either in support or engaged in assisting the Royal Engineers in digging new communications trenches. During this time they were subject to hostile artillery fire and lost men accordingly. Then they withdrew from the battlefield, marching in easy stages to Dellettes, arriving on 27th June. After a period of training, rest etc. the battalion moved on to Ypres, taking over from 10/Cheshires in the Ramparts on 9th July 1917.

3rd Battle of Ypres

The Messines action formed a curtain raiser for the 3rd Battle of Ypres, whose main purpose was to capture the Belgian ports in enemy hands. To a considerable extent this was thought necessary to deprive the German submarines of their bases close to Britain, and relieve the pressure on the Royal and Merchant Navies. It was also thought necessary to distract the Germans away from the French sectors due to the unrest amongst our ally's soldiers following the failed Nivelle offensive earlier in 1917.

In the entry for 10th July (covering 10th-14th) it is noted that the battalion suffered from a new form of gas - mustard gas. The symptoms are described in detail in the War Diary: "This gas destroyed the sense of smell and its presence was very difficult to detect but for its first symptom, continuous sneezing. In many cases several hours later vomiting and affectation (sic) of the eye ensued." Lt. Wait refers to this in a letter home[7]:

> We have not been having too good a time lately - working parties nearly every night. The Bosche[8] have been trying a new sort of gas shell on us which affects men in different ways. Personally I have lost my voice which is rather a nuisance and can only talk in whispers.

The battalion was used to provide labour for trench repairs, burying dead animals and other unpleasant duties, all under constant threat from shell fire. This continued until the end of July, with some respite at Reninghelst for training and rest.

By 31st July the 5th Army was able to deliver its attack along the line from the Zillebeeke-Zandvoorde road to Boesinghe. 25th Division was in II Corps' reserve on the left of the Corps' front. II Corps itself was on the right of the

---

7 *Letter to Mother dated 22nd July 1917.*

8 *Normal spelling is 'Boche'.*

5th Army's front just to the south of Ypres. The idea was that after the 8th Division had captured its objectives the 25th would then pass through them to attack the next set of objectives. The first objectives were not reached, with 30th Division being held up by fire from well-fortified positions. The 8th Division made more progress, reaching the outskirts of Westhoek. On the following day (1st August) the 1/Wilts were called upon to relieve 1/Sherwood Foresters on Westhoek ridge, a task they managed with some difficulty owing to heavy shelling. On 2nd August mention was made of the rain and mud that was to become the hallmark of the whole battle. Conditions made it difficult to re-supply the men in the front line, and the whole process was exhausting for those involved. Added to that was the shelling from British guns falling short. On a more positive note the War Diary records the success of its snipers against the enemy, speculating that a relief was taking place at the time. Perhaps the Germans were equally affected by the conditions, tempting them to leave the comparative safety of communication trenches. Active patrolling the following day secured an enemy position some 50 yards in front of the line, whilst the Germans shelled the front line generally. The early morning of the 4th was marked by an enemy counter-attack, but this did not affect the 1/Wilts position - although short shooting by our artillery did. Finally, on 5th August the battalion was relieved by men of the 2/R. Irish Rifles and 9/Loyal N. Lancs - the relief being made difficult by the conditions and disposition of the men. Hot baths, a change of clothing, cinema performances were a welcome break from the front. All box respirators were replaced as they had been used for more than the 40 hours for which they were designed. This battle in particular made heavy use of gas shells.

On 10th August an attack on Westhoek ridge and village by the 25th Division was renewed. This attack was successful. The 1/Wilts were in reserve, and placed under the temporary command of 74th Brigade. Being in reserve was not an escape for the dangers of the battlefield, as they were involved in supplying men on the front line during a period of intensive and accurate artillery fire which the Germans were able to deliver from behind the ridge. Relief came on the night of 12th/13th August, and for the rest of the month the battalion was engaged upon training and rest/refit in the Busseboom-Steenvorde area. Even this break did not afford a complete respite, since an air raid on 20th August caused 3 casualties. There was a short spell back at the front in the vicinity of Westhoek, and then back out of the line until early October.

1/Wilts officer group, mid 1917. Maj. Ogilvie back row 5th from left.

Bethune - Bapaume

The battalion then moved to Bethune (4th October), billeting in the Ecole Des Jeunes Filles - surely a felicitous move given the conditions faced by those who continued the battle further north - Passchendaele. The line of front held at this period centred on Givenchy, and it was a quiet sector. The War Diary for this period is sparse on information, although it mentions patrols, trench improvement work, and some bombardments. Out of line training, resting, sport and refitting interspersed with manning the front line filled their days.

During late November and December 1917 the 1/Wilts took a circular tour south and arrived in the area of Bapaume, east of the Somme battlefield. On 11th November, a full year before the end of the war (and on the day Ludendorff met to discuss the German offensive for 1918) the War Diary records working parties, concerts, training, reorganising companies into 3 platoons, and for the first time in nearly a year a battalion Officers' Mess. Less happily Lt. Swayne[9] records a sad fatality:

> It was rather rotten luck on one of our officers, White[10] by name, who was just back from leave, where he had got married; he got shot through the head by a sniper. His girl being married and a widow in 10 days.

During the period in the line and in reserve, trench routine was followed, with regular patrols being sent out. More digging and carrying, and improvements to roads and trenches helped keep the battalion occupied during the winter. Boxing Day 1917 saw them hard at work. They managed to bury 500 yards of cable, and the following day "one of the best performances in digging ever done by the Battn." was recorded. This pattern continued into early 1918: feverish activity by the 1/Wilts and their fellows in 25th Division, apparent inactivity on the German side.

On 3rd February 1918 yet another organisational change took place. The Brigade was reorganised into 3 battalions, the 8/Loyal N. Lancs being disbanded. The losses at the 3rd Battle of Ypres were not being replaced as a matter of policy set by the Prime Minister (Lloyd George).

---

9 *Letter to parents, dated 11th November 1917.*

10 *2/Lt. Sidney Herbert White, died aged 25, buried in Grave: III.J.19 Bethune Town Cemty. Married to Mary E. White of 84, Rue Africaine, Brussels.*

During February training began to start again at Achiet le Grand, near Bapaume. This included firing with gas masks on, and training for the stretcher-bearers, now at a strength of 32 for the battalion (or about 5% of the men).

Chapter 5 - From the Brink of Defeat to Victory

The German March Offensive - Battle of Bapaume

The 1/Wilts were still at Achiet le Grand on 21st March 1918 when the Germans launched their 'St. Michael' offensive. Although not in the front line, the battalion was shelled by the enemy and suffered casualties. It was part of the German artillery plan that not only the forward positions be shelled, but also the 'battle zone' behind. At 11.30a.m. the situation at the front caused the 1/Wilts to be ordered forward. By night time they occupied the army line running from the east of Beugnatre and Fremicourt. It was here that Capt. R. F. J. Hayward[1] won the battalion's only V.C. The citation ran:

> This officer, while in command of a company, displayed almost superhuman powers of endurance, and consistent courage of the rarest nature. In spite of the fact that he was buried, wounded in the head, and rendered deaf on the 21st, and again had his arm shattered on the morning of the 23rd, he refused to go down even though he received a third serious injury to his head on the afternoon of the 23rd, until he collapsed from sheer exhaustion.
>
> Throughout the whole of this period, the enemy were attacking the company's front without cessation, and this officer continued to move across the open from one trench to another with absolute disregard for his own personal safety, concentrating entirely on reorganising his defences and encouraging his men
>
> It was entirely due to the magnificent example of ceaseless energy of this officer that many most determined attacks upon his portion of the trench system failed entirely.

On the following day the Army line was consolidated, although in the evening the Corps line (Vaulx- Morchies) fell to the enemy. A day later things seemed to go well for the Wiltshire men. German bombardments occurred, but their attacks were beaten off - the Lewis gunners did "great execution" amongst their foes. There was no respite at night as the enemy were out trying to cut the wire for their next assault. Next day things did not go so well, with

---

1 *Later promoted to Lt. Col. and commanding a P.O.W. camp in World War 2. His medals are on display in the Wardrobe Regimental Museum, Salisbury.*

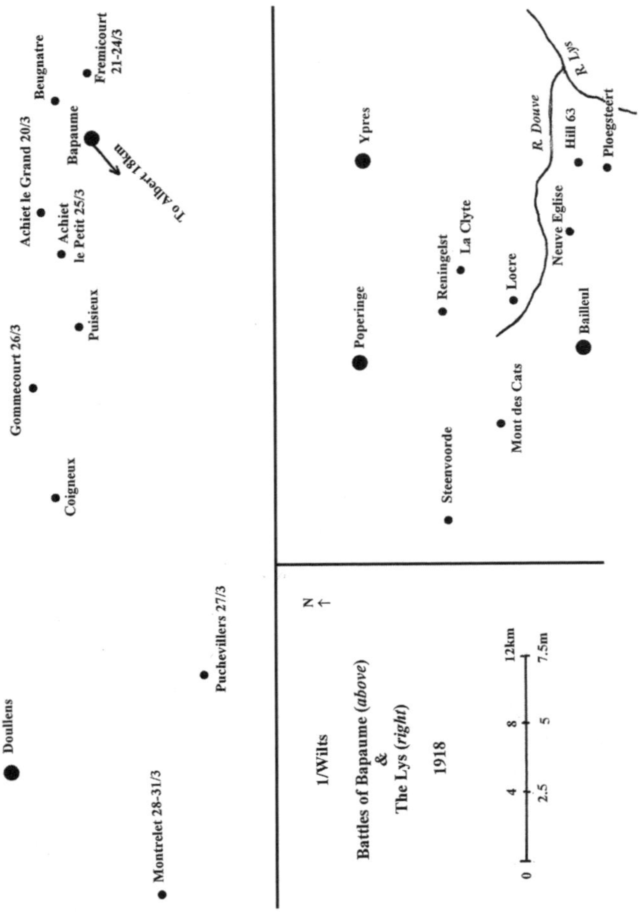
Doullens
Montrelet 28-31/3
Puchevillers 27/3
Coigneux
Gommecourt 26/3
Puisieux
Achiet le Grand 20/3
Achiet le Petit 25/3
Bapaume
To Albert 18km
Beugnatre
Fremicourt 21-24/3
1/Wilts
Battles of Bapaume (*above*)
&
The Lys (*right*)
1918
N
0
4
8
12km
2.5
5
7.5m
Steenvoorde
Mont des Cats
Poperinge
Reningelst
La Clyte
Locre
Bailleul
Neuve Eglise
Ypres
R. Douve
Hill 63
Ploegsteert
R. Lys

Map 8

Capt. R.F.J. Hayward, V.C.

well-directed artillery fire aided by German aircraft, and our own artillery falling short and causing casualties. In the late afternoon the Germans came forward, but their attack did not meet with success. However, an urgent message was received to break off the engagement and retire. At the same time the units to the right of 1/Wilts were forced to retire leaving that flank 'in the air'. Attempts to stem the retirement of these troops were initially successful, although they were subsequently wiped out by machine gun fire. The battalion moved back to Achiet le Petit, mustering at 3 officers and 54 ORs - casualties over the past few days having been 413. Map 8 shows the area of the Battles of Bapaume and the Lys.

Here, again, the 1/Wilts held their line but found their flanks exposed. Command seems to have broken down at Brigade level, for Lt. Col. Ogilvie on his own initiative decided to take the battalion to Puisieux. On the night of 25th/26th March they marched to Gommecourt. They were back at the Battle of the Somme starting point. On 27th further marching, this time to Puchevillers where at least they were able to sleep at night in a camp. Then to Montrelet, where the battalion was organised into 2 companies, each with 2 platoons. From there the battalion marched and used trains and motor lorries to reach Neuve Eglise near Bailleul. For his leadership during the battle Lt. Col. Ogilvie was awarded a second bar to his D.S.O. (a very rare distinction), and other officers and men had their courage recognised - all this on top of Capt. Hayward's V.C.

Battle of the Lys

The March offensive brought the Germans close to the vital position of Amiens, the capture of which would have cut the British Army off from their French allies. Their advance faltered towards the end of March, but meanwhile the Allies had agreed to place the strategic direction of the Western Front in the hands of Marshal Foch. Fresh French troops and an exchange of British Divisions led to the removal of exhausted units. Thus the 25th Division were now back in the Ploegsteert area, having been refreshed and reinforced (mainly by 19 year olds). However, the shortage of suitable material for N.C.O.s was felt. The divisional sector (described by Kincaid-Smith) was about 7,000 yards long, between the River Lys to the River Douve, with the 7th Brigade on the left. They were now part of the IX Corps of Plumer's 2nd Army, and were on the right flank of that Army. On 9th April the Germans attacked the area held by the Portuguese, south of the line held by the 25th Division. This was the start of the 'Georgette' offensive, made against the line north of the line attacked during 'St. Michael'. 1/Wilts

War Diary reported a quiet day. This was to change on 10th, when the German attack through the early morning mist was preceded by a heavy bombardment. They used the infiltration tactics employed during the previous attacks and were thereby able to penetrate between units and cut them off. The War Diary records that 'A' Company was cut off, and that after resisting attacks for more than 1 hour 'D' Company and the remainder of the battalion took up a line (Zambuk Post-Ultimo Crater) which they held for the rest of the day. The *Official History*[2] records that "The company of 1st Wiltshire (7th Bde) in La Basse Ville (just south of Warneton), in the front line, held out until 8.35a.m., when the few survivors, having expended all their ammunition and bombs, were forced to surrender". It goes on to record that attempts by the 7th and 57th Brigades to retake Ploegsteert Wood were driven back, but that "further enemy advances were stemmed due to good artillery cover (aided by good communications due to buried signal cables), short range fire and a lifting mist."

Further German assaults forced the Division back, the War Diary for 11th April simply recording that the enemy's capture of the Catacombs and Ploegsteert Woods forced the battalion to withdraw to the vicinity of Ravelsberg. The *Official History* tells us more. "The enemy made strenuous efforts all day against IX Corps". The fighting on 10th April "had left 7th Brigade in a pronounced salient at St. Yves, which represented a 2 mile face to the south along the north edge of Ploegsteert Wood as far as Hill 63, whose flat top afforded good observation." The 1/Wilts were one of the units holding this face. The Germans were able to make advances on the flanks of 7th Brigade, and their position looked increasingly precarious. The Brigade were ordered to fall back to high ground west of Neuve Eglise and the 'Catacombs' - a series of caverns dug into the west face of Hill 63. The *Official History* points to confusion here in orders, and a cancellation of the retirement order in the late afternoon. However, the enemy were able to close around the Catacombs and Hill 63 position. Two companies of the 1/Wilts who had held Zambuk post during 10th and 11th April were able to reach the new position near Neuve Eglise, led by Capt. Priestley. The Catacombs position, housing the battalion Headquarters of both the 1/Wilts, 10/Cheshires and 4/S. Staffs, was overrun by the enemy. Amongst those captured was Lt. Col. Ogilvie, who had served with the battalion since 1914. Again, the 1/Wilts were reduced to a remnant - the *Official History* stating that it stood at 70 men of all ranks, and pointing to interference from Divisional Headquarters as being responsible for an "unnecessary disaster".

---

2 *1918 Vol 2.*

Kincaid-Smith's work tactfully omits this criticism, and the War Diary is too brief to explain all the activity during the action.

The following day (Friday, 12th April) saw what was left of the 1/Wilts in their new position near Neuve Eglise, but they were marched to Bailleul in response to an incorrect report that the Germans had broken through at that point. They then had to march back to a position near Crucifix Corner where they came into action. More fighting took place the following day, with counter attacks against the enemy incursions around Neuve Eglise. The War Diary for 13th April mentions a counter attack against the Germans, and heavy enemy artillery fire. The *Official History* tells us that the salient around Neuve Eglise was abandoned during the day due to penetration by the enemy. Kincaid-Smith says that the enemy were ejected from Neuve Eglise that day, and the position held until troops withdrew just before daybreak on the 15th.

On 14th the War Diary shows a day in the trenches with the battalion subject to heavy artillery fire. The *Official History* says that the 7th Brigade, formed into a composite battalion from its remnants, was subject to heavy bombardment, and that just before midnight the order was given for the 25th Division to be relieved. The War Diary confirms that this took place during the following morning. Four days later the battalion reached Steenacker, where they started to reform. The War Diary for the 19th pays tribute to the remarkable work done by its transport section:

> During the period from the 1st to this date the Transport was brigaded under the command of Major Blew, 1st Wilts Regt and moved back almost daily in accordance with the requirements of the situation without suffering any loss either in horses or personnel. It is also noteworthy that rations, water, SAA[3] and supplies of all kinds never once failed to reach the fighting line with success and regularity, this fact contributing not a little to the remarkable defence put up by the Battn. Transport difficulties were increased by the fact that each shift involved in all cases a second journey to bring along blankets and other essential stores. This was successfully effected and no stores whatever had to be abandoned to the enemy.

---

3 *Small Arms Ammunition - i.e. for rifles, Lewis guns etc. Not artillery shells.*

The 2nd Battle of Kemmel

By 23rd April, and now in camp north of Poperinge, the battalion was brought up to a strength of 21 officers and 760 ORs - the officers all coming from the Durham Light Infantry. Thus, by 25th April, the battalion was deemed ready to go into action once more at Kemmel. The French were holding Kemmel Hill, and they had first been attacked on the 23rd. This was beaten off, and a follow-up attack was made by the enemy, resulting in the German capture of Kemmel village by the morning of the 25th. A recapture by the 22nd Corps with the support of 25th Division was ordered. At 3a.m. on the 26th the counter-attack started. Progress was impeded by the rain, which had started at mid-night, making the Kemmel Beck a more difficult obstacle. By 5a.m. the 7th Brigade had reached its objectives and had captured men and machine guns. The French, who were to advance on the right of the British, failed to make their objectives. This, according to the War Diary, led to the 1/Wilts and their colleagues being withdrawn to trenches 1,000 yards north of La Clytte. The next day (27th) they moved to shelter trenches near Reninghelst. On 29th they received a false report that the Germans had broken through on the right, and they were required to prepare defensive positions. That day the battalion was placed under the orders of the 39th French Division. On the 30th they received (and had countermanded) orders to support French attacks.

During the early part of May the 1/Wilts occupied reserve trenches, and on 4th May Lt. Col. Furze took up command. Up to 8th May the battalion rested and trained out of the forward area. On 9th May the battalion moved to Arcis-le-Ponsart, where the 25th Division was to take up a position with IXth Corps in a quiet sector of the line in the Chemin des Dames area. They were part of the 5 British Divisions considered to be so exhausted by the earlier German offensives as to require time to refit and retrain.

Casualty ratios during the 1918 German Advance

Fig. 3 below draws on figures published in Kincaid-Smith's *'The 25th Division in France and Flanders'*. It tabulates the (K)illed, (W)ounded and (M)issing for the period October 1915 to the end of 1917 (just over 26 months - including the Battle of the Somme and Messines), and for the actions in March and April of 1918 - the German advance. They make for interesting comparisons.

During each of these periods just over one quarter of all officer casualties were likely to be fatalities. The proportion of O.R. casualties reported as fatalities was just under half that of officers during 1915-17, and lessened considerably during the German offensive. The proportion of wounded for both officers and O.R.s in 1915-17 stood at around three quarters for each. For March 1918 the wounded proportion for officer casualties drops to 58% i.e. just over one half. For O.R.s it drops to 20%, only one quarter of the 1915-17 proportion. The number of 'Missing' rises dramatically in 1918, although with the officers just single numbers can make a significant difference to percentages. The obvious difference is that in 1918 the Germans were advancing, and therefore able to capture men whether wounded or not, and it would be more difficulty to keep tally of fatalities where they lay in captured ground. The fact that the proportion of officer fatalities remained fairly constant suggests either that they were more likely to be exposed to danger during the German assaults, or that they were less likely to surrender - and that the men were more likely to surrender once their officer had been killed.

Some N.C.O.s were clearly able to take the place of their officers. Kincaid-Smith records some of the more notable awards for gallantry in the 25th Division. Cpl. Cole for example, on 26th April, led his platoon into action during a counter-attack on Kemmel, and led the withdrawal in good order. All this was done in the absence of any officer or senior N.C.O. He was awarded the M.M.

	Officers			**Other Ranks**		
	K	W	M	K	W	M
1/Wilts 10-10-15 to 31/12/2017	23	63	3	230	1467	186
	26%	71%	3%	12%	78%	10%
25th Division	270	858	44	3683	17949	2337
	23%	73%	4%	15%	75%	10%
1/Wilts as % of Div. total	9%	7%	7%	6%	8%	8%
1/Wilts Feb.-March 1918	5	11	3	34	83	294
	26%	58%	16%	8%	20%	72%

25th Division	34	105	40	284	1391	1549
	19%	59%	22%	9%	43%	48%
1/Wilts as % of Div. total	15%	10%	7%	12%	6%	19%
1/Wilts 9-4-18 to 04/05/2018	5	5	6	24	173	482
	31%	31%	38%	4%	25%	71%
25th Division	43	170	57	486	3596	3350
	16%	63%	21%	7%	48%	45%
1/Wilts as % of Div. total	12%	3%	11%	5%	5%	14%

Battle of the Aisne

As part of IXth Corps the 1/Wilts now came under the command of the French 6th Army under General Duchesne. The Chemin de Dames ridge was held by both British and French units, with the 25th Division being used as a Corps reserve. They were first centred at Arcis-le-Ponsart, some 15 miles behind the front line. Their first day there was spent in cleaning up and making a prompt start on training.[4] A Divisional School was opened at Coulonges, and training continued through to 22nd May. On the following day the battalion moved forward. Gen. Duchesne was adamant that, faced with the prospect of a German attack, more troops should be pushed forward to the front. This policy ran counter to the experience of the British, who were now familiar with the German tactics. They had found that front positions should be lightly held and main forces held some way back to absorb and counter-attack. By mid-May it was becoming apparent that such an attack was imminent. From 24th-26th May the 1/Wilts were at Prouilly, on the east bank of the River Vesle. Map 9 shows the area fought over during the weeks following.

On 27th May the attack commenced, with the now familiar orchestrated bombardment starting at 1a.m. and continuing through until 5a.m. This proved successful for the Germans, and at 7.30 the 1/Wilts were ordered forward to cover the retirement of the troops in front. Later that morning

4 *Cpl Mohan's diary (see Part 2) describes the march to Arcis and the days following.*

(10.15a.m.) the battalion was moved further forward to hold a line at Bouffignereux. This line was held until about 5.30p.m., although during this time the battalion H.Q. came under shell fire, and movement was restricted due to sweeping enemy machine gun fire. The Germans had crossed the River Aisne and the adjoining canal at Maizy. This success, and a similar enemy advance from Pontavert, meant the loss of Bouffignereux and the rushing of the battalion H.Q. The whole position became untenable, and the 1/Wilts retired in small groups, fighting rearguard actions as they went. The War Diary notes that the battalion came under 8th Division during the day, and that parties of men were reorganised and sent to fill gaps in the line. The *Official History* records that during the retirement the 1/Wilts went south and the 2/S. Lancs of 75th Brigade southwest, creating a gap. Attempts were made to fill this gap by the 130th Field Company R.E., but this failed. The action had split apart the 7th Brigade, with the greater part moving to a defensive position between Bouvancourt on the north and Pevy on the south. The 1/Wilts with some other elements were due south of Bouvancourt (*Official History*). This formation was commanded by Maj. Cannon of 1/Wilts.

On the following day (28th) the enemy followed up their attack and the battalion, with other units, continued a fighting retirement southwards. Kincaid-Smith mentions actions at Pevy and again to the north west of Prouilly. By nightfall Maj. Cannon's men were south of the River Vesle at Branscourt. Again, Kincaid-Smith gives us additional detail. He records Maj. Cannon's unit holding the enemy up south of Prouilly that night. The 1/Wilts may have suffered loss and been fragmented, but clearly they still had plenty of fight left in them. On 29th the War Diary tells us that an enemy advance to the left through Fismes caused a re-alignment of the front, facing northwest to meet this threat. A more modest advance by the enemy led to a short backward step southeast to Sarcy. Transport crossed the Marne, but otherwise the battalion began to collect its various strays together. Two days later the War Diary reports that the battalion was well to the south of the River Marne at Beaunay.

On the 1st June (and somewhat confusingly) the War Diary has the battalion back up on the River Ardre where they were split into three:

- one force commanded by Maj. Cannon, and adjoining the 4/KSLI,[5] and north of the River Ardre, east of Sarcy;

---

5 *King's Shropshire Light Infantry.*

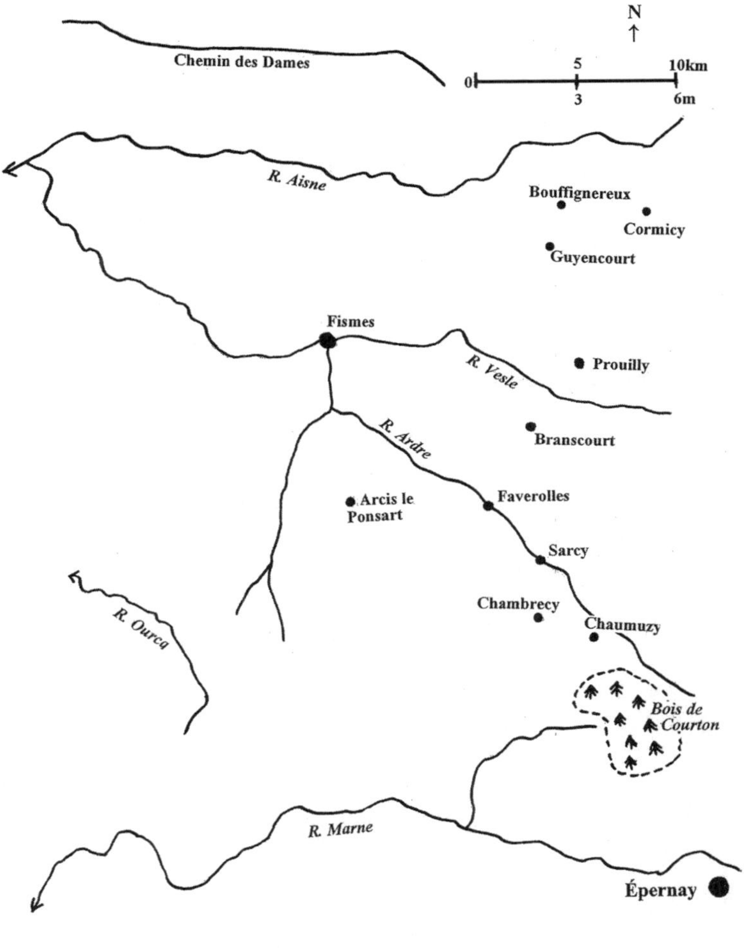

1/Wilts The Battle of the Aisne May-June 1918

Map 9

- a second force under Capt. Parkes, fighting with the 8/Gloucesters, west of Chambracy; and
- the HQ and transport back at Beaunay (and over 30km - as the crow flies - away from the main body.

From then until 17th June the now combined force was occupied in defending the line and beating off the odd (and by now less determined) attacks by the enemy. On that date (17th) the battalion was relieved by the 1st Btn. 19th Regt. of the Brescia Brigade, Italian Army. The 1/Wilts acquired a new C.O. on the 19th (Maj. J. T. Bridges D.S.O. of the Worcestershire Regt.) and on 21st June they joined the 110th Brigade of the 21st Division. This Division, too, had been in the thick of the action during the German offensives, and had been in front of the 25th Division holding the line on the 27th May.

The Advance to Victory

The new Division, with the 1/Wilts, moved to the vicinity of Gamache (between Dieppe and Amiens) where they could rest, refit and train. The War Diary goes through a blank period. On 2nd July there was a move to Raincheval, just behind the old Somme battlefield. From then until the 19th the battalion was left in peace to continue its training, with a new C.O., Lt. Col. G. B. C. Ward D.S.O., arriving on 7th July. He was to take the battalion home again in 1919. During the training the War Diary reports that the battalion suffered from an influenza epidemic. On 16th-17th a route march to Acheux Wood (a matter of some 9km as the crow flies- but route marches do not always take the direct route) in hot weather proved to be hard going, with many of them falling out en route. One is forced to conclude that these soldiers were not of the same standard as those who marched with the 1/Wilts during the hot August of 1914. The battalion, along with the rest of the British Army, was making do with what manpower was available.

On 24th July there was a move forward to the area of Engelbelmer, close to the German positions. The line in this sector ran north-south just to the west of Albert. Normal trench duty seems to have been resumed in this area, with references to shelling by the enemy and casualties resulting. Maj. Cannon left to take up a post in the 59th Division. Information was received (14th August) that the Germans were withdrawing from their positions, and some intensive patrol work was required to ensure that their movements were monitored so as to be effectively exploited. Posts were established at Thiepval village, close to the scene of the battalion's action in 1916. These posts served as sally ports for the patrols. The enemy were still alert enough to capture one such patrol on the south edge of Thiepval Wood, where 2/Lt. Dowson was cut off. The battalion lost nearly 30 men on that occasion. Further south, the allies were counter-attacking in force. On 8th August - the 'Black Day' of the German army - the allies had advanced southeast against a German salient pointing at Amiens. This advance made a dent in the German line just to the south of Albert, rendering the enemy position opposite the 21st Division less attractive, although by the 11th this attack was brought to an end. The B.E.F. had learned that initial success only led to further complications with supply and bringing up artillery. Maps 10 and 11 show the progress of the 1/Wilts as the Allied armies pushed the Germans back.

The 21st Division and the 1/Wilts worked their way forward. They crossed the River Ancre on 24th August, when they caused an anxious moment for their Brigade commander (Brig. Gen. Hanway R. Cumming[6]) who had 'lost them' in the advance. Fortunately the battalion was able to look after itself and when Brig. Gen. Cumming re-established contact they were found to have taken their intended objective near Le Sars. By 1st September the battalion had taken Beaulencourt, just south of Bapaume, having come by way of Miraumont, Le Sars and Eaucourt. The Germans of course, contested these advances. An annex to the War Diary describes the attack on Beaulencourt in detail:

> The Battn marched to its forming up position and formed up on the road for N4c5.5 to N4d3.7[7] in the following order:-
> Front line B Coy (under Capt C H Gaskell) on the right
> A Coy (under Capt H B Brown, MC) on the left
> Support line C Coy (under 2nd Lieut F G Pitt) on the left
> D Coy (under Capt E J Brewer) on the right
> At 2.0a.m. a creeping barrage was put down on the line N11d0.0 to N12a0.0 and remained there for 20 minutes. At the same time heavy Artillery bombarded BEAULENCOURT and the high ground to the east of it.
> The Battn went forward under the barrage in extended order and attacked the village.
> Battn HQ were established in the trench at N10d9.0.
> The village was strongly held by enemy machine guns but the Battn attacked with such determination that the opposition was overcome and by 5.30a.m. the village was in our hands.

---

6 *Detail in 'A Brigadier in France'.*

7 *Trench map references.*

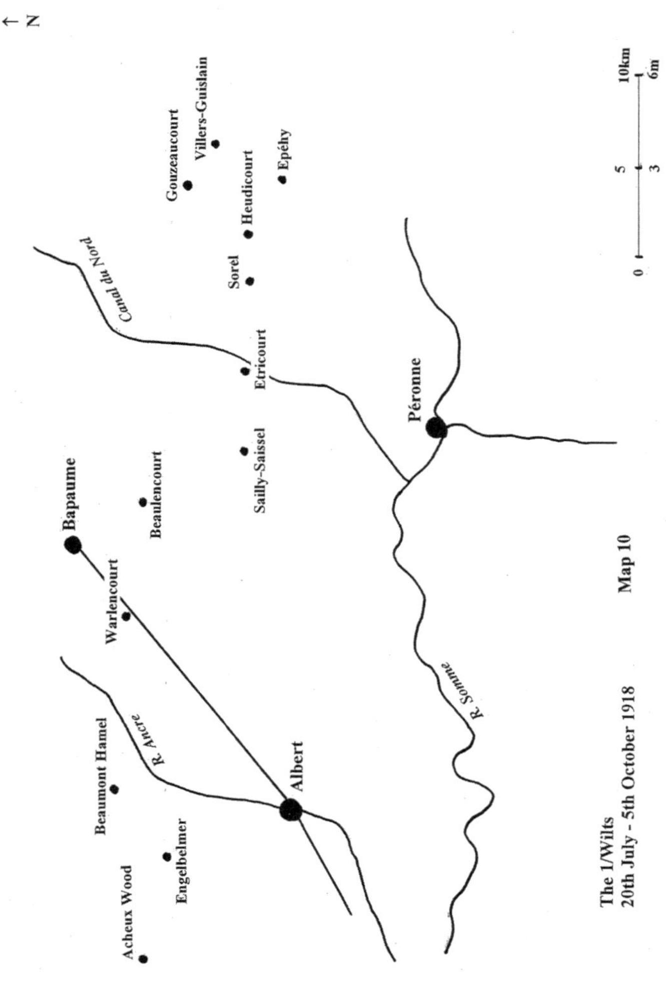

N
Villers-Guislain
Gouzeaucourt
Heudicourt
Epéhy
Sorel
Canal du Nord
Etricourt
Péronne
Sailly-Saissel
Beaulencourt
Bapaume
Warlencourt
R. Somme
R. Ancre
Beaumont Hamel
Albert
Engelbelmer
Acheux Wood
0
5
10km
3
6m
Map 10
The 1/Wilts
20th July - 5th October 1918

Map 10

A Coy at once consolidated in the trench from N18c2.7 to N17d9.4 and D coy come up on its right and held a series of Platoon Posts from N17d.9.4 to N17d0.5 and C Coy after mopping up the village took up a position in reserve in the sunken road in N17c. B Coy pushed forward on the left flank and held a very advanced position in N18c until on the 1/2 Sept when they withdrew to reorganise in the village. Our right flank was protected by a section of M Gs from a Coy 21st M Gun Battn who took up a position from N17d5.3 to N17c5.2.
At 6.30 the enemy attempted a counter attack under cover of a smoke barrage but it was easily repulsed.
The following war material was captured in the village:-
2 Field Guns (Damaged) 21 Light Machine Guns
2 Light Field Pieces 5 Anti Tank Rifles
2 Heavy Machine Guns
Approx 100 Prisoners were captured including 4 officers
Our Casualties were:-
Killed: Officers 2nd Lieut A W Healy ORs 17
Wounded: Officers 2nd Lieut F G Pitt ORs 41
Missing: Officers Nil ORs 1
After the village of BEAULENCOURT had been captured the enemy resistance entirely broke down and the neighbouring villages of LE TRANSLOY and VILLERS-AU-FLOS were soon taken and the Divisions on either flanks swept forward after the enemy.

In *'A Brigadier in France'* Cumming adds a little more detail:

The plan of attack was that the 6th Leicesters on the left, with their left on the Bapaume Road, and the 1st Wilts on the right, were to form up in the valley running South-West from the Bapaume Road and immediately West of Riencourt, and move parallel with the Road, preceded by an enfilade artillery and machine-gun barrage, and capture and occupy the village. .....

The attack on Beaulencourt was completely successful: as a flank attack, it obviously took the enemy completely by surprise. The 6th Leicesters and 1st Wilts. swept through the village and, after some very heavy fighting in which good use was made of Lewis guns and trench mortars, the whole village was captured and a position consolidated round the Eastern and South-Eastern portions of it.

Cumming also notes that in addition to capturing men and material a more or less intact field hospital was also captured. Counter-attacks by the Germans were beaten off by the 1/Wilts. There followed a short spell in reserve until ordered forward on the 7th September to Etricourt. A German deserter revealed plans for an attack against the Brigade on 13th September, so both sides commenced an artillery barrage at the same time, 9.45a.m. At 10a.m. the Germans came with their flamenwerfers, gaining them a footing in the area of Chapel Redoubt. A platoon of the 1/Wilts was quickly organised to eject them.

Attention was now focussed on the Epéhy area. On 16th September orders were received (according to Cumming) for "an operation on a big scale and on a wide front, to take place on the morning of the 18th." This involved an advance by the 62th Brigade to capture enemy trenches between Vaucellette Farm and Peiziere, with 110th Brigade (with 64th Brigade on their left) going through to take the positions south and west of Villers Guislain. The 110th would then push on east to protect the flank of 12th Division, who would tackle Epéhy to the south. The 1/Wilts took their position, but were compelled to retire as the 12th Division failed to take Epéhy. The War Diary is not particularly helpful, with many gaps in the narrative. However, there is an appendix at the end of the entry for the 30th September that sheds more light on the events of the 18th:

> At 8p.m. on the 17th the Battn marched from its Bivouac at Valley Copse (V.9.a2.0) to the FINS - NURILL road (V17d7.1.) and at that spot picked up a Taped Track leading S of SOREL - le - Grand and HEUDECOURT to a point on the railway W 23a5.2. At the commencement the track was clearly lined, the night fine and the marching was good. At 10.20p.m. the Bde sent orders for the Battn to halt and clear the track so as to allow a Battn of the 2nd Inf Bde to pass through. This Battn passed through at 1.50a.m. 18th. It had commenced to rain, the track was laid across a sunken road, the men had great difficulty in crossing and there was considerable delay. At about 700 yds from the railway the tape ended, the track marked by posts only and they at wide intervals: it had become very dark and the Coys kept on missing the track.
>
> The Battn formed up facing E on a line 3 yds W of (unclear) in W24a. The 6th Battn the Leicestershire Regt was to the S of the Railway and on the same alignment. The 62nd Inf Bde was drawn up in front. At 5.20a.m. the Barrage opened, the 2nd Inf Bde attacked the Trenches on

> the Western and Eastern slopes of the High Ground in X13.c.X 19a and c. The Battn and 6th Leicesters followed them closely until they reached the sunken road and railway cutting in W24b and X19a. When the 63nd Inf Bde completed its capture of this objective, the Battn advanced forward by a creeping Barrage the objective being LIMERICK TRENCH X21b7.2 to LEITH WALK X15d5.9. On our right the 6th Leicestershire Regt on the left 64th Inf Bde. The capture of the objective was to be carried out as follows, A and C Coys under cover of the Barrage capture MEATH POST with bombing parties and artillery support to Coys to work in towards and establish touch with troops on our flanks. B Coy mop up LINNET VALLEY and reinforce its front line. D Coy in support.
> The following actually took place, A & C Coy captured MEATH POST and worked outward according to plan. The two on our flanks and not come up - our bombing partied were driven back and MEATH POST was counter attacked in strength. A & C withdrew and took up a position in MEATH LANE and the ridge in X15a X20b X21a. B Coy cleared LINNET VALLEY and reinforced the front line, D Coy in support in road X20b 7 d: with Battn HQ in same place.

Resting and routine front line work continued until 29th September when the 110th Brigade was to have attacked a trench line south of Gonnelieu. Intelligence was faulty, as the enemy still held positions thought to have been evacuated. The attack did not take place. On 3rd October the Brigade took over the whole divisional front since the 62nd Brigade was withdrawn. By now the 1/Wilts were in the vicinity of the Canal de St. Quentin (Canal de l'Escaut). Regular patrol work probed the German positions. Two days later it was discovered that the enemy had abandoned their positions east of the Canal and the Brigade moved quickly, crossing at Bantouzelle. By noon they were in possession of the Hindenburg Line. On the same day the War Diary records the battalion's strength - 34 officers, 855 O.R.s, 48 horses and 3 mules. From now onwards the numbers of horses and mules becomes a regular feature of the diary.

On the 7th the battalion turned south and attacked the trenches on the Beaurevoir line, after having started from the vicinity of Rancourt. Their move during the night of 7th/8th October was not an easy one due to the darkness and the amount of wire encountered. However, they were in place in time to mount their attack, which was successful. Casualties were incurred through enemy machine gun fire, and 'A' Company was unfortunate enough to have strong wire impede their advance, leaving them vulnerable to hostile

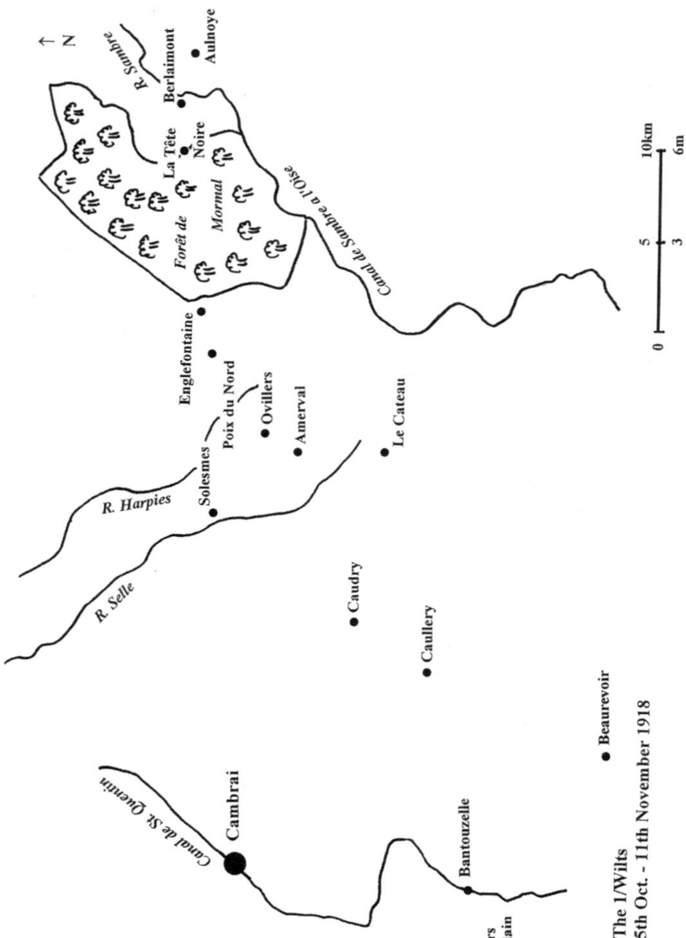
N
R. Sambre
Berlaimont
Aulnoye
La Tête
Noire
Forêt de
Mormal
Canal de Sambre a l'Oise
Englefontaine
Poix du Nord
Ovillers
Amerval
Le Cateau
Solesmes
R. Harpies
R. Selle
Caudry
Caullery
Beaurevoir
Cambrai
Canal de St. Quentin
Bantouzelle
Villers
Guislain
0
5
10km
3
6m
The 1/Wilts
5th Oct. - 11th November 1918

Map 11

artillery fire. From 10th to 22nd October the 110th Brigade rested, reorganised and trained at Caullery, battalion H.Q. being set up at 12, Rue de Sac. They were within 6km of the ground they held at Caudry just over four years previously during the Battle of Le Cateau. On 12th October the tally of men and livestock was: Officers 32. O.R.s 767. Horses 49. Mules 3 - a reduction of 2 officers and 88 men in just over a week, although they had acquired a horse and managed to keep all their mules. Capt. Swayne, by now Company Commander for 'D' Company, indicates the extent to which training was necessary, given the influx of new men[8]: "We have been training and reorganising, but I have not got the Coy anything like straight yet."

Towards the end of October (22nd) the 1/Wilts were back to the attack, making a route march during that day via Neuvilly to take up positions to attack at Ovillers. They were marching in exactly the opposite direction to that taken during the retreat from Mons to Caudry, and just a little to the south of the route they took then. The whole 3rd and 4th Army fronts were involved in this forward movement, and the plan was to take a number of objectives in 'bounds' by successive waves of units. Just after midnight the battalion were assembling the men in preparation for the attack. A mist formed, and they moved forward and out of the mist to where tape was being laid. At this point the enemy artillery opened up causing casualties and disrupting the preparations. At 2a.m. on 23rd the British artillery barrage started, and the objectives were rushed. In the capture of Ovillers 'A' and 'C' Companies went forward to the next objective but the rest of the battalion got lost in the dark. Further advances were made on 24th October, with the battalion marching to Poix du Nord, although enemy machine gun fire held up the advance of the 64th Brigade, and so the Wiltshires withdrew. All these tactics were in marked contrast to the costly attacks made earlier in the war. On 26th it was back to Ovillers for few days before returning to Poix du Nord on the 29th. Here they stayed until the late afternoon of the 2nd November. According to Brig. Gen. Cumming[9]:

> the area being shelled very heavily at times. Poix itself received considerable attention, mainly between dusk and dawn, with a certain amount of gas. The billets were good in Poix, but it was hardly a safe place of residence.

---

8 *Letter to parents, 20th October 1918.*

9 *'A Brigadier in France'.*

At the beginning of November (2nd) they moved by route march to Amerval. The War Diary has a copy of the battalion orders for this march. The following day the 1/Wilts retraced their steps and moved to Engelfontaine on the edge of the Forêt de Mormal. On the 5th the 62nd Brigade was able to cross the River Sambre and the 1/Wilts then moved through the Forêt de Mormal to Le Tête Noire on the east side of the forest. Next day they advanced on Berlaimont, on the west bank of the River Sambre. The opposite side, with the village of Aulnoye (where the battalion detrained on its advance to Mons, 16th August 1914), was strongly held by Germans, and the bridges destroyed. However, the 1/Wilts were able to effect a crossing, but were unable to extend their foothold on the east bank. By 11a.m. the 32nd Division had captured Aulnoye Station, and so a flanking movement round the right of the village was attempted. The enemy withdrew leaving the battalion to take their objectives and establish their H.Q. in the brewery. On 7th November the battalion advanced a little further east until they came under heavy machine gun and artillery fire. They held their line until 11.30a.m., when the 64th Brigade moved through to capture the line along the Maubeuge-Avesnes road (the N2 on modern maps). On the following day the battalion marched back to Berlaimont. It was here that they heard that the Armistice was to take effect at 11a.m. on the 11th. The war was over.

A flavour of the last few weeks of action is given by Capt. R. Swayne.[10]

> I have at last time for a few lines, as you can see we have been very busy again, and have marched miles after Master Hun.
>
> We have had some very rough moments and it has been very interesting and exciting. It would have been almost enjoyable but for the fact that it poured with rain, and we were never dry wading through marshes and all sorts. For sheer fatigue and hardships it is an eye opener for me what you can do if you try, in the way of doing without sleep and grub; though we are always better off for the latter than the former.
>
> We are very well off for billets now; and the freed civilians can't do too much for you. The Hun has not time now for organised destruction, and is too busy shelling troops and places of military importance to blast villages off the map as he used to be, just bumps them a little usually the Church.

10 *Letter to parents dated 9th November 1918.*

In the villages we took during these last days we really had a most triumphal progress, people running after us with coffee and hailing us with cheers as deliverers and real excitement. …….

All the civilians tell us awful tales of Hun cruelty to English prisoners. Working under fire, half starved and often no boots; if any civilians offer help they are made prisoners and the soldiers beaten.

Chapter 6 - Demobilization

Shortly after the Armistice took effect the battalion marched to Beaufort. The War Diary records the messages of congratulations from Army, Corps, Division and Brigade commanders. It remains blank for a number of days, until 28th November, when fresh troops joined that battalion. On 30th the number of officers, men and horses is recorded, with the officers listed, together with the awards made. Early in December (3rd) H.M. King George V visited the Divisional area together with the Prince of Wales and the future King George VI. Lt. Col. Ward, the 1/Wilts C.O., was acting Brig. General in command of 110th Brigade and was presented to His Majesty. On the 14th December 14 miners left for home - evidently not bound for Wiltshire, but desperately needed elsewhere for their skills.

In the middle of December the battalion moved away via Berlaimont, Vendigies and Inchy before embussing for Clairy Saulchoix, just to the south west of Amiens. Just before Christmas a party left to collect the Regimental Colours left behind at Le Marchant Barracks, Devizes, in 1914. They returned on 31st December. The War Diary continues into 1919, but where there are entries they are mainly concerned with the numbers leaving for the Corps Concentration Camp (a term not having the ugly connotations acquired later) or for the Army of Occupation. Many officers and O.R.s joined the 2/5 Gloucestershires who were to be based in Germany. On 8th March the battalion marched to Bovelles, which was to be their home until 5th April. Then they marched to Bouchon on the River Somme, 13 km south east of Amiens. There, on 23rd May, they received orders to make their way to England. Five days later (29th), after a brief stay at Harfleur, they embarked at Le Havre with 5 officers and 60 men. The battalion had been in France and Belgium for 4 years 289 days.

Fig. 4 below shows the change in numbers from Armistice Day onwards. At first the battalion was reinforced, since it would take some time to get the machinery for moving men into reverse gear. And, of course, it would be dangerous to reduce men too quickly given the number of men and munitions still available to Germany. It was only from the middle of January 1919 onwards that numbers started to drop. From the end of February onwards the battalion dropped from company size down to that of a platoon by the time they left France.

Date	Officers	ORs	Total	Difference	Horses	Mules
16/11/1918	32	682	714		53	
30/11/1918	34	747	781	67	55	
01/12/1918	34	747	781	0	55	4
14/12/1918	38	739	777	-3	51	4
31/12/1918	41	821	862	85	51	4
01/01/1919	41	823	864	2	48	7
11/01/1919	40	832	872	8	48	7
17/01/1919	38	754	792	-80	48	7
25/01/1919	36	641	677	-115	48	7
31/01/1919	36	547	583	-94	48	7
08/02/1919	35	498	533	-50	47	4
15/02/1919	30	436	466	-67	37	4
22/02/1919	30	435	465	-1	33	4
28/02/1919	27	221	248	-217	33	4
15/03/1919	27	171	198	-50	9	0
22/03/1919	27	149	176	-22	7	0
31/03/1919	17	119	136	-40	6	0
15/04/1919	10	98	108	-28	0	0
22/04/1919	10	92	102	-6	0	0
30/04/1919	10	92	102	0	0	0
10/05/1919	8	90	98	-4	0	0
13/05/1919	7	86	93	-5	0	0
21/05/1919	7	72	79	-14	0	0
29/05/1919	5	60	65	-14	0	0

Fig. 4. 1/Wilts Demobilization November 1918 - May 1919

Conclusion

Robert Graves[1] describes a conversation held in the instructors' mess at the 'Bull Ring' training camp just before the Somme offensive. They were discussing the merits of the various units in the B.E.F. One of the conclusions reached was that "English southern county regiments varied from good to very bad." There is sufficient evidence from the record of the 1/Wilts to suggest that it was a 'good' regiment. It took part in most of the battles of the war, repeatedly held to its line, and its officers and men won many honours. When forced to retire it was because their flanks had been compromised. Although it missed out on much of the Passchendaele (3rd Battle of Ypres) campaign, it had the misfortune to be caught up in the three major German attacks of 1918. In each of these attacks the battalion lost considerable numbers, yet it quickly assimilated reinforcements and went on to perform with distinction. After returning to England the 1/Wilts were brought back up to strength and resumed their pre-war role of policing the Empire.

Perhaps one of the most remarkable features of the 1/Wilts story is the career of Lt. Col. Ogilvie.[2] He joined the battalion in the field in December 1914 with the rank of acting Corporal. Just over 2 months later he was commissioned. He was mentioned in despatches in December 1915 and assumed temporary command of the battalion in July 1916. A month later he was awarded the Distinguished Service Order after having been wounded in action. In October 1917 he was acting Brigadier General - this just two and a half years after being commissioned. He was awarded two bars to his D.S.O., and survived the war although the last few months were spent as a prisoner of war. Lt. A. J. S. White remembered him in his writings:[3]

> The 1st Wiltshires were a fine battalion. They were commanded during my time by an outstanding man named Ogilvie, a barrister in his 30's, a very brave man and a great leader. He had enlisted as a private at Devizes in 1914 and, though obviously officer material, had insisted on his rising steadily through the ranks of Corporal, Sergeant and so on. He ended the war as a Brigadier.[4]

---

1 *'Goodbye to All That'*

2 *Born 1884, educated at Rugby and University College, Oxford. C.B.E., 1947. Died 27th March 1961 at Leiston, Suffolk.*

3 *Lecture Notes.*

4 *White's recollections regarding ranks does not tally with the War Diary - but Col. Ogilvie's outstanding record cannot be disputed.*

After the war the surviving officers met annually for dinner at the Restaurant Frascati in Oxford Street. They were known as 'Ogilvie Dinners'.[5]

Lt. White has other interesting observations on the morale and 'glue' that kept men together as a fighting unit:

> In these appalling conditions the troops, both officers and men, were surprisingly cheerful. There were several reasons for this. Companionship means a great deal to young men (and indeed to others) and many of these men now had for the first time the advantage of being surrounded by a large number of other young men: a few, of course, did not relish being in such a crowd, but most did. To quite a number soldiering had even been welcomed as a relief from boredom or uncertainty or Domestic unhappiness in civilian life. Then there were the periods of rest behind the lines which gave much enjoyment merely by contrast with what (had) gone before.

Many more regiments have achieved higher prominence in the history of the Great War, and references in the war literature to the 1/Wilts seem strangely few given the battalion's record on the Western Front. The personal diaries, letters and recollections cited in this work are valuable sources of information on the war generally and on life with the battalion in France and Belgium. The War Diary signposts us to a remarkable story that deserves to be remembered and more widely known.

---

5 *There are several menus and group photographs of these dinners in the papers of Lt. R. Swayne, held by the Imperial War Museum.*

Part 2 - Three Personal Diaries

Warfare from an individual participant's perspective often differs from the more 'broad brush' picture given in histories of the conflict. But it is the individual accounts that help us visualise what it must have been like to have been there, and give personality to the individuals who took part in the struggle. The Imperial War Museum holds three diaries kept by members of the 1/Wilts.

Capt. C. H. Gaskell's covers the period from 11th August 1914 to his return to England for convalescence after 18th October 1914; Sergeant H. G. Perry's from 2nd September 1914 to 2nd January 1919; and Corporal T. G. Mohan's from 11th April 1918 to 23rd September 1918. The following is a summary of their contents.

My Experiences in 1914 August to October – C. H. Gaskell

The early part of the diary describes Gaskell's attempts to join the army just after the outbreak of the war. Using his motor-bike he visits Bulford Camp, Salisbury, and Devizes. He was finally directed to Weymouth and the 3/Wilts under their C.O., Lord Heytesbury. Here he seems to have had some sort of rudimentary training in drill, trench digging and lectures on various topics. On the 30th August, and with just over a fortnight's experience of the army, he was posted to France in command of a detail of 92 men.

This band of reinforcements landed at St. Nazaire (the usual disembarkation ports being evacuated due to the German advance). The British troops, still being a novelty in those parts, received a warm welcome from the inhabitants. The men had to bivouac several miles from the town, and as more troops arrived the camp took on a more permanent air. The entente cordiale was preserved by excluding the troops from St. Nazaire. Tommy showed his baser side during this period, when Gaskell was supervising the movement of supplies at the docks. Leaving his men to go and draw cash for their pay, he returned to find that they had broken open cases of liquor and half of them were very drunk. One died and several were hospitalised following their experience. They got off lightly, however, with just a fine – due to the camp commander's delight on hearing of the victory on the Marne.

On 17th September the Wiltshire party, with other reinforcements, entrained to join their units. The journey proceeded at a snail's pace, giving the soldiers an opportunity to receive gifts of wine and cognac from the French. The Wiltshire men, chastened by their experience at St. Nazaire, stayed sober. Others did not, and some simply fell off the train to be left where they fell. The Irish contingent took to fighting each other with bayonets. All in all, the officers had their hands full during the journey.

Finally they made it to Braine and Gaskell was welcomed into the 1/Wilts. On hearing that he had been a land agent, the 2nd in Command, Maj. Barnes, said "By Gad, you'll be damned sorry this time to-morrow that you were ever fool enough to chuck it to come out here!" Hardly inspiring words from a senior officer to a young one – and perhaps indicating an attitude that explains Maj. Barnes' swift removal back to base a few days later. That night Gaskell marched up to the trenches, crossing the Aisne by a pontoon bridge constructed by the Royal Engineers. On the following morning he met the men coming in from the trenches.

> They looked awfully pale and worn these men. They nearly all had beards - officers and men - and were literally covered in mud and wet through. They had had no rest since the battle of Mons and no chance of a wash or shave. One of my fellows sang out "Are we downhearted," and there came the caustic reply "No but you bloody soon will be."

Gaskell was assigned to 'A' Company, and spent the next few hours in being inspected by the C.O. (Col. Hastead), breakfasting on cold ham, biscuits and jam, and constructing a shelter. This idyll was interrupted by enemy fire, and Gaskell with 30 men was sent to man the trenches[1] and whilst moving up along a slightly sunken road they came under shellfire (marked by xxxxxx on Gaskell's sketch map –see Map 12 - drawn later from memory). Some men were killed, and the enemy were able to gain a temporary advantage by calling out in English "Stop firing. You're firing on your own men." and later, when their nationality became clear, pretending to surrender. Good advice was given by the Sergeant Major "don't ever trust 'em. Shoot every damned one that shows himself." During the same action the British artillery fired upon a large group of Germans who had surrounded some of the Wiltshire men. Lt. Gaskell had seen a demonstration of modern warfare stripped of its glamour.

German incursions were repelled by the battalion, with 2nd Lt. Roseveare (Old Marlburian) leading a "brilliant charge" but getting mortally wounded in

---

1 *It must be remembered that 'trenches' were not the intricate and interlinked affairs associated with the later stages of the war.*

the process. The C.O. was also wounded as the Germans had got as far as the battalion H.Q. before being driven back. Major Roche then took command. All of this took place on 20th September according to the War Diary.

The next day (21st) was spent in burying the dead - including some 80 Germans. The 1/Wilts took 150 casualties (dead and wounded) in the action. That night Gaskell was sent on outpost duty with 10 men, a few hundred yards further from the trenches. They were posted in front of a detachment of the 12th Lancers, who were warned of their presence. During the night they were fired upon by the enemy, drawing counter fire from the Lancers. Luckily none of the Wiltshires were hurt. They beat a hasty retreat to the trenches once fire died down and, although relieved at the outcome, Maj. Roche sent them back for a further watch.

On 22nd Lt. Gaskell with others sat in their dugouts carving names of the dead on crosses made out of sticks and bits of ration boxes (and being shelled into the bargain). That night they were relieved, and marched back to Braine - a difficult march made pleasant through Capt. Stoddart's[2] exposition on the stars above. On arriving Gaskell changed into pyjamas before turning in, but an alarm in the middle of the night meant dressing and getting ready to meet the enemy. It was a false alarm, and acting on the principle that lightening does not strike twice the pyjamas were attempted again the following night - with a further alarm, making him and his fellows late for the start. Again a false alarm, but future nights were spent fully dressed! The stay was otherwise pleasant, with the locals making them welcome. One interesting observation at this time was that the cavalry stained their horses with Jeyes' Fluid to make them less conspicuous. One further, and quieter, spell at the front followed, with Gaskell spending time collecting snail shells (he was clearly knowledgeable on this topic).

Then followed the withdrawal to the left flank of the Allied armies. This involved a long march by stages to Le Maux where they entrained. The train crawled along, stopping frequently, and the men had to be discouraged from getting out and buying things en route. By the 10th October Gaskell was at Pernes, which had good shops with limited merchandise thanks to German looting. Their hosts proved inhospitable, and charged extortionate prices.

Cautious progress was made on the following days, since they were approaching the enemy once more. Gaskell records days spent at La Couture,

---

2 *Killed in action, Neuve Chapelle, October 1914. Awarded the Legion d'Honneur for bravery during Aug. 1914.*

some 3 miles west of Neuve Chapelle. On his last day there the Divisional commander, Maj. General Hubert Hamilton, was killed.

> Everyone was extremely sorry as he had been awfully brave and energetic and was with us day and night and had spoken to me several times. His body was brought down to La Couteau[3] to be buried in the Church yard and there happened to be an attack by the enemy that night and 'A' Coy were called out to be ready to go up in support. We were lined up along the wall of the church yard while the funeral was being conducted just inside, and there was very heavy shelling and tremendous rifle fire and bullets coming down into the village street and striking the walls and the road with a flash. It was an impressive funeral altogether I thought.

The Germans were being pushed back, and on the 16th October the 1/Wilts relieved the South Lancs. in a wood just SE of Neuve Chapelle. Eventually the men reached their position, and settled down for some sleep. Gaskell records sharing a barn with a fellow in charge of a Pom Pom gun, who had wounded a Brigadier whilst attempting to down an enemy aircraft:

> We told him we wished it had been our own Brigade Commander MacCracken [sic](who was unpopular for good reasons) and we asked him to keep further details 'til morning.

The morning brought a continued advance, with the Wiltshires making short rushes from cover to cover ....."I remember thinking this was very much pleasanter warfare than the sample we had on the Aisne." On the next day (18th October) the 1/Wilts were ordered to advance with the KOYLIs[4]. The diary gives a detailed account of this day's action, its confusion, and the events leading up to Gaskell's wounding. The last section of the account describes his evacuation back to England.

Gaskell rejoined the battalion at the end of January 1915 and was promoted Lieutenant on 2nd February. He was wounded again in April, in the hand, and went back on duty after a short period. On 13th December he was made temporary Captain. During 1916 he had several periods away from the battalion due to ill-health. On 1st July 1916 he was attached to IX Corps as

---

3 *Evidently means La Couture. Maj. Gen. Hamilton is now buried at Cheriton, St. Martin, Kent.*

4 *King's Own Yorkshire Light Infantry.*

1/Wilts
Sketch Map of Position
20th/21st September 1914
(from sketch made by Capt. Gaskell later)

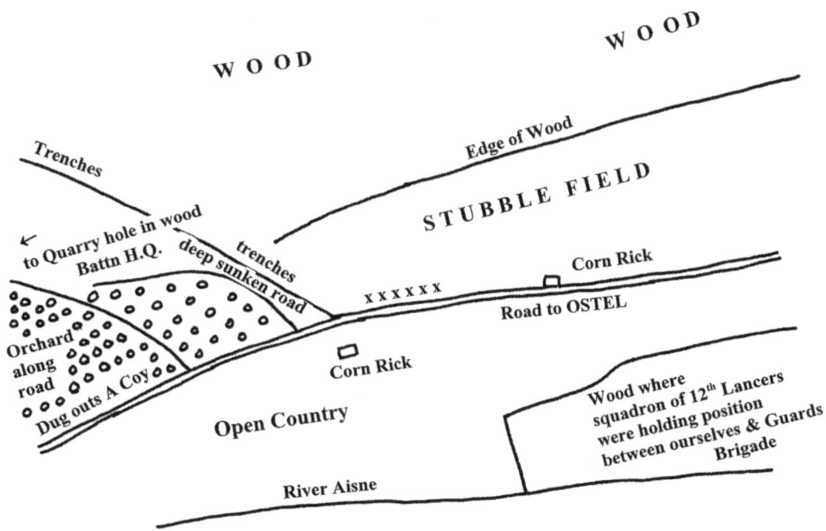

Map 12 - 1/Wilts Sketch Map of Position 20th/21st September 1914

'Agricultural Officer'. More illness followed in 1917, and on 1st August 1917 he was made Transport Officer for 7th Brigade. Further hospitalisation was required during 1917/18 for various reasons, although he was able to rejoin the 1/Wilts in the field in August 1918 and took part in the battles of the final advance. On Armistice Day Capt. Gaskell became sick and went to the Field Ambulance.[5] Along with the rest of the armies on the Western Front, his war was over. He rejoined the battalion on the 11th December, and was released for demobilization on 11th February 1919.

Diary of No. 10366 Sergeant Hubert George Perry

Born 20th July 1895, died 6th August 1967. In a preface to the typed version of Sergeant Perry's diary there is a brief summary of his career. It also mentions his medals, including the 'Mons Star', although this is not possible as his diary indicates that he first landed in France in January 1915.

Sergeant Perry's diary starts on 2nd September 1914, and continues (with gaps) through to 2nd January 1919. For some of the time he was with the battalion transport, and therefore not so exposed as his comrades. However, even these duties did take him to the front line, and the positions occupied by the 'support' teams were by no means free from enemy attention.

The diary generally consists of fairly short entries giving the location and one or two points of interest. The first few entries concern his enlistment and training - he was fortunate in spending Christmas Day 1914 in Weymouth Workhouse. The humour of the situation was not lost on him!

After landing in France Perry is sent to join the battalion at the front on 13th January 1915. He records that Sgt. Pullman was shot in the head whilst standing next to him. The War Diary records this as being a 'quiet day', with only one man wounded. On 4th February he is admitted to hospital with frostbite in the foot, and enteritis. This keeps him away until the 19th August 1915, when he rejoined the battalion at Ouderdon. Four days later he was in the trenches to

> spend about 6 days of horror there. Many casualties. No fires allowed except 3 men at a time allowed to "bully up" at the bottom of the crater[6] nevertheless Gwilliam, into whose section I have fortunately managed

---

5 *i.e. the Divisional medical facility.*

6 *At Hooge.*

to get, “Bullies up” in the dug out by the aid of wood cut up fine as matches.

On 29th August what appears to have been a significant breech of discipline seems to have occurred:

> Casey Barnard[7] arose from his dugout one night during the past tour and walked along the trench and put about ten men under arrest for various offences, some serious, some trivial, some imagined. Sgt. Bryce and Sgt. Sainsbury were among them. During the past tour too, A Coy. had an unfortunate incident which resulted in many of their N.C.O’s being swopped with other Coys.

On 1st December Perry is made Quartermaster’s orderly. This seems to have been a fortunate move. On 24th January 1916 Perry records:

> Whenever there’s a general inspection I generally manage to find out that the Canteen required beer from Baillent.[8] Try my hand at riding the Q.M.’s horse with Crook’s connivance, afraid several times went to bed rather inebriated.

He also records the famous barn burning episode of 3rd April 1916 - “great excitement, Court of enquiry etc. etc.”

The diary records detail of the battalion’s work in the early days of the Somme action.

> *2.7.16.* The Somme Battle has now opened in all its fury. We leave Varennes and march to Hedauville. Arriving in Hedauville midday, we stay here up to 10.30 p.m., when the Bttn marches off to stay the night in Avelay wood. The transport leaves at the same time and drags along all night at the rate of half a mile an hour - blocks and stoppages, via Bouzincourt, till we get to Martinsurt wood, where we arrive just as the cold grey dawn is breaking. I bribe a man of another Regt. nearby for a drink of tea and lay down but unable to sleep a wink - nor is anybody - owing to 4 guns, 4.7’s, barking away not 50 yards distant from us.

---

7 *Presumably Capt. Cary Barnard D.S.O., who joined the battalion in October 1914, and commanded the battalion for a few weeks in April/May 1915. Overall he seems to have had a distinguished war record.*

8 *Probably means Bailleul.*

3.7.16. The Battn. goes into the line, and I go wandering up there too, endeavouring to find them, and eventually do so, via Campbell Avenue and Authville. I come back, only to have to go up there again on another errand. When I get back I am warned to proceed up there again at night ration carrying, but I protest, and eventually Marquan goes, - I am dead beat.

During this tour in the trenches Lt. Col. Brown[9], S/M Lester, Lt. Morris[10] and many other old friends are killed, also Lt. Terry[11] (Adgt.) and R/S/M Parker wounded.

5.7.16. Battn. still up there, and we hear they have lost half their strength in casualties, Major Ogilvie has before this gone up to take command in Lt. Col. Brown's place, and he with the Doctor and one other are the only officers who emerge. In B. Coy., no sergeants left and a corporal brings them out acting as Company Sergeant Major. We shift the Transport back another 800 yards into a hollow where we stayed about 4 days. During this tour self had a lively time crawling through the Russian 'Sap' at one end of which I last saw S/M Lester and Lt. Morris alive.

9.7.16. About this time I have one of the most agonising nights of my life. We shifted via Aveluy and Albert late at night up on to the Albert-Bapaume Road, just on the Albert side of La Boisselle, and had a terrible time trying to keep up with the transport in the dark, as we went across tracks which were a foot deep in heavy mud and I with a loaded bicycle found it awful, I carried bicycle, rifle pack and all for about a mile on my shoulder. Arriving up on the Albert-Bapaume road we stayed beside the Regiment[12] and I helped to put out rations in the early dawn of the 10th., as Smith was back at the last lines with the G.S. waggon. A blind shell nearly finished me off by falling down near us and skidding along the ground with the nosecap off, emitting sparks and fire.

---

9 *War Diary gives 5th as date killed, Commonwealth War Graves Commission database gives 6th.*

10 *Killed on 7th July.*

11 *Wounded on 7th July.*

12 *The War Diary gives Usna Hill as the position.*

10.7.16. We leave this spot, after staying there about 6 hours and come back just on the hill behind Albert, leaving the Regiment there. We hear they have one or two casualties through shells falling among the cookers etc.[13] So they get into the trenches already existing there. They furnish digging parties in La Boiselle etc., whilst there, and shortly afterwards move up into the line.

We find on arriving at our lines on this hill beside Albert, that the A.S.C.[14] were too funky to come up there with rations, and had dumped them at Bouzincourt, so after waiting for them all day, we finally had to send back our own transport to fetch the rations. Thus do the A.S.C. "Feed the troops in the firing line" as they are always boasting. Good heavens!

Whilst on this hill we are constantly troubled with long range shelling, and have to take refuge during the night in a trench near by.

Subsequent entries show that out of the line the battalion (or at least the transport team) had quite an enjoyable time of it . Near his 21st Birthday he receives a cake from home, and they have a "pleasant time" at Beauval (18th July 1916). Then, on 12th September 1916 Perry records having 13 "enjoyable days" at Coulonvillers, and he goes into Abbeville most days for beer and canteen stores. On 27th October he is promoted Lance Corporal. On 11th March 1917 he is at Sercus "where we spend an enjoyable 8 days." Life seems even better on 5th May 1917, when they got to Esquerdes "where we stayed a fortnight and had an excellent holiday. I slept in a bed!" The battalion had their photograph taken and their bayonets sharpened. The 1/Wilts then took part in the Messines battle, although transport stayed at Revelsberg. On 15th December 1917 Perry is made full Corporal. A gap occurs in the diary, but on 6th March 1918 Perry is deputising for the R.Q.M.S.[15]

The German advances of 1918 are covered in the diary, and although further back with the transport, Perry has a trying time of it with the shelling and handling the retirements. The diary gives more detail on the third encounter

---

13 *No casualties reported that day in the War Diary, although a shell kills one and wounds three on the 12th July.*

14 *Army Service Corps.*

15 *Regimental Quartermaster Sergeant.*

with the Germans - the Battle of the Aisne. In an entry dated 29th May 1918 he gives a clear picture of the chaos that resulted from this German attack:

> Shifted from Goussancourt at 9 a.m. Self went to D.H.Q.[16] at 6 a.m. to try and ascertain where they were moving to, so that we could follow them, but snubbed for my pains. Capt. Webber[17] then goes to the G.S.O.1[18] but meets with a like fate. Whilst we are here we are informed that we are attached to the Y Divn.[19]
>
> We travel via Villers Agron to a point near Olizy and arrive midday. We put up in a little clearing on the edge of a wood, - have a good feed, a cup of wine, and a short rest. We hear that Capt. Hawkins[20] was killed at Rosnay. Shift at 4 p.m. via Olizy, Romigny and Chatillon to 'Vaudieres' where we arrive at 6 p.m. and spent the night there. Self went during evening to Vernenil and all over the shop to find the A.S.C., but no success. By the way whilst in a little clearing near Olizy our ration limbers are turned back and we are informed that we are no longer to ration them. We ourselves are "Floating about space" without a Commander.

After various adventures, Perry and the transport got back with the battalion on 20th June 1918 when they entrained for Mille Bosc. The next day he puts up his third stripe. Sgt. Perry, evidently an adaptable old soldier now, settles down to make the best of it - breakfasting well at an hotel on one occasion, with Benedictine and a cigar to follow! For the next few weeks the battalion and its transport are engaged upon routine defence work, but towards the end of August they are ready to take part in the final advance and defeat of the enemy. Unfortunately his friend Gwilliam is killed at around this time.

The entry for 6th September 1918 has the battalion "into the Ramparts, Ypres", rather confusing as the War Diary says they were moving from

---

16 *Divisional Head Quarters.*

17 *Takes over command of transport 5th April 1918, and one of the few officers to survive the earlier German advances. Fortunately he was still with the battalion at the end of the war.*

18 *General Staff Officer 1 - Normally a Lt. Col. Probably Lt. Col. R. T. Lee, D.S.O.*

19 *21st Division whose badge was 3 sevens arranged rather like the Isle of Man device.*

20 *Not mentioned in the War Diary or Casualty list.*

1/Wilts Sergeants with French family outside billet/estaminet.

Beaulencourt to Sailly-Saissisel, and this fits in with the general context of the 1/Wilt's movement at this time. The battalion was at Ypres Ramparts on that date in 1915 (and again in July 1917), and so there is probably a mistake in the year. A few entries later Sgt. Perry's diary has us back on track with the advance, and relates the progress made by the battalion. The Armistice is noted briefly, and Perry is detailed to go with a party to Clairy Saulchoix to organise billets - a difficult task involving wrangling with the inhabitants. Otherwise he spent his time in "drinking and playing billiards". His last entry (2nd January 1919) notes that "Officers censorship removed. Sign your own envelopes."

My War Diary - Corporal T G Mohan

This is the longest of the three diaries and is in printed form, dated Christmas 1919, although no other publishing details are given. It was evidently written after Mohan's return to England and is based upon a rough diary he kept whilst on active service. Mohan was a very religious man, and this clearly comes across in his narrative - at times it seems to echo Bunyan's *'Pilgrim's Progress'*. It is a very useful document in that it covers a wide range of topics detailing the soldiers' everyday life in and out of the front line. Mohan evidently saw service prior to the date of the diary. On 22nd April he says "Nearly all of us who were N.C.O.s together (now Privates) in the 34th at Exmouth , managed to get into the same Company" (on joining 1/Wilts).

Mohan starts his account from the time he and his comrades are 'warned' for service overseas. On 11th April 1918 the Colonel, Lord Heytesbury,[21] had them on parade and made a farewell speech before presenting each man with a shilling. They were taken by train to Shorncliff and marched to Folkestone before embarking for France. After passing through one of the camps at Etaples, the men made their way towards the battalion via reinforcement camps. At Godwearsveldte he was startled by a huge explosion.

> We learnt that it was a twelve inch gun firing.....It was an enormous thing mounted on a railway truck especially constructed for it, which had 32 wheels! Attached to it were closed ammunition wagons and a big railway engine.

---

21 *He is the same commander under whom Capt. Gaskell trained as a young officer in 1914.*

> The big twelve inch shells were loaded automatically from the ammunition wagon, and then dropped on a miniature railway on the gun platform, and were pushed along by five or six men right into the breech of the gun……. the wagons were then disconnected and the engine pulled them away about 100 yards. All the men got off except the one who was to fire it….The man who was to fire the gun stood on the reinforced part above the breech and pulled a cord! How can I describe what followed! Involuntarily we closed our eyes while a mighty blast of wind seemed to slap us in the face and lift our clothes about three inches from our body all round.

On 22nd April Mohan meets up with the 1/Wilts at Jock Camp (near Poperinghe) . The battalion had just come out of the second of their encounters with the German advances of 1918. Mohan reports that:

> out of 800 of the Battalion who went into action, besides reinforcements received during the action, only 80 came out. The Band and all the Bandsmen were captured complete. Drafts of men were sent straight from the base, and joined the Battalion but were not even known, or placed in any Company but were killed or taken prisoners almost at once - many of them boys of 18!

Mohan was made No 1 (fires the gun) of No 4 Lewis Gun section and "made the acquaintance of Captain Brown[22] (then Lt.) whose - well the less said the better! I ought not to say anything as he was very decent to me." A few days later (25th April) the battalion was back in action in the area of Kemmel. Mohan was selected to form part of the 'B' team. The action was fraught with difficulties, and the 'B' team saw the withdrawal of the heavy guns and observation balloons as a bad sign. On the 4th May the main battalion rejoined the group.

The 25th Division then moved to the 'quiet' sector in the Champagne region. Mohan has some vivid descriptions of the train journeys and marches. During one such march the customary 10 minutes rest after 50 minutes marching was ignored by the officer.

> I know that I felt quite done, and the men began to get angry and to shout out a Cockney phrase "What abaht it?" meaning to imply "What

---

22 *Capt. H. B. Brown M.C. Joined 1/Wilts in October 1916. Awarded bar to M.C. in September 1918. Left battalion in October 1918 and was eventually invalided to England with influenza and bronchial pneumonia.*

about a rest." This annoyed Capt. Brown (who always rides a horse and has nothing to carry) and he ordered the Company to march at attention. This was the last straw and was mere brutality. Capt. B. turned out to be nothing more than a bully and a coward. We all felt very bitter about it and the men's hearts were near to mutiny ..... I for one felt so indignant that I inwardly refused to do it and just kept my rifle slung over my shoulder. It was so dark that no one noticed it, but Capt. Brown found one or two who were doing it and he ordered them an hour's pack drill - which is marching about for an hour with full pack on.

Mohan did admit that by giving this unofficial punishment rather than formally charging them, Capt. Brown was sparing the men from having an adverse comment in their records. He also considered that the officers thought they were close to the final destination and did not think a rest worthwhile. However, by this means the battalion reached Arcis-le-Ponsart on 10th May 1918. Shortly afterwards the battalion got a new C.O.[23] and Lewis gun officer[24] - these 'new brooms' "were keen and liked to see us at work". Mohan, regarding himself as something of an expert on the Lewis gun, did not always agree with the new officer's views on the weapon. Moral generally does not appear to have been high within the 1/Wilts at this time. Football in the afternoon was made compulsory (hitherto voluntary) so that some men simply pretended to play, leaving others to run around covered in sweat. The officer in charge (unnamed) "said that it was a pity we ever came back from the last stunt, and the Germans ought to have had the lot of us." One man wrote home a letter giving his candid opinion of the officers. This, of course, was subject to officer censorship. Capt. Brown gave him 14 days field punishment.

On 26th May 1918 it was clear that something was 'up', and the Germans would start their attack. Once again Mohan was part of the 'B' team. His diary gives a detailed account of the days that followed as seen from the viewpoint of an ordinary soldier. However, dates are a little questionable - the German attack is given as starting on 27th in the War Diary and other sources. Rather like the retreat of 1914, the 1/Wilts and the other units in the area were pressed back over the following days, usually under intense enemy shellfire. Men from the various Divisions became mixed together and were liable to be

23 *Presumably he means Lt. Col. Furze, D.S.O., M.C. who joined the battalion on 3rd May 1918.*

24 *2/Lt. H. Stanway joined the battalion in the field on 22nd April 1918, apparently from the Durham Light Infantry.*

attached to any unit on the spot that needed them. Relief for Mohan came on 30th May.

> At last we came to a big wood which was really the forest of Rheims.[25] Here we were destined to spend many days. There had been a charcoal burner's hut here where we found some sacks...So we ate what remained of our rations. Then we chose a nice sheltered spot, and gathered several bundles of brushwood which we found about there, and piled this up to form a square wall to keep off the wind a bit. Then we got our feet into a sack which reached up to our armpits, and with a few sacks over us we soon went to sleep about 8.30 p.m. and we didn't wake again till 9 a.m.

A little later Mohan tells us that the blisters on his feet acquired during the German advance were to stay with him until he got to England in September. Otherwise he and his comrades were involved in watching the line and keeping out of enemy sight during daytime. On 6th June another heavy artillery bombardment with gas and high explosive shells was experienced, but the Germans were unable to break through.

> Every time a shell burst very close we would shrivel up into our holes, and then look over at one another to see that no one was hit. We felt very unsafe as our heads were not properly protected. We could not have our whole bodies under cover as the holes were not long enough. The stretcher bearers were very busy and worked like heroes, running about in the open without any thought or fear for themselves. A lot of the fellows where Heaps and I were felt so unsafe that whenever there was a lull they made a dive for some more protective cover. We preferred to stay where we were. I never agreed with running about during shelling as one is quite likely to run into a shell.

At last, on 17th June, the Division was relieved by the Italians. Their stay in the area was over. Marching and train journeys took them to Peas, where they arrived on 19th June to get a dressing down from Capt. Brown for unclean buttons and muddy puttees. Pte. Mohan was told of his promotion to acting Lance Corporal, and had to endure "a long sermon from the Major unfolding to me the great responsibility, and wonderful privilege of the high honour which was about to be conferred on me..." A few days later, on 28th, Mohan

---

25 *Perhaps the Bois D'Eclisse referred to in the War Diary.*

was promoted to Corporal. On 3rd July the commander of 21st Division, Maj. Gen. Campbell, inspected the men.

> It was unique in many ways. He wouldn't have all the ceremony of presenting arms when he arrived, which a Brigadier General would have had. He had us all sitting down and we were not allowed to rise on his arrival. He addressed us as 'Gentlemen' and said how proud he was to have us in his Division. He concluded by telling us that we could do nothing by ourselves, but only by the help of God, and finally he urged us to pray, and not think that such a thing was foolish or to be despised. What a power for God such a man's witness can be!

Shortly afterwards Mohan was invited to apply for an officer's commission, but turned down the offer. The 1/Wilts moved up to the vicinity of their action during the Somme battle in 1916. The final advance was to begin. The steps forward are described by Mohan, and the German power of resistance is made clear - the advance was difficult and dangerous. The men were under almost continuous enemy shelling, and gas was a nuisance. On 4th September, whilst at Beaulencourt, Mohan sees the field hospital mention in Cumming's memoir, and notices that the Germans were using bandages made of paper (since cotton was in short supply). On 15th September he remarks upon the effect of German aerial bombing which he thought worse than shelling.

> ...some of those huge aerial torpedoes which are used are over eleven feet high and make a hole which would require a long ladder to get out of. Such an explosion is fearful, and the shock would kill anyone within a radius of a hundred yards or more. The horror of these things is inconceivable to those who have not seen its effects.

Cpl. Mohan's war was shortly to come to a premature conclusion. On 19th September he went in search of other members of his platoon in order to bring them back prior to being relieved by men of the 33rd Division. He appears to have lost his way and encountered a group of enemy soldiers. Whilst trying to get away from them he received a bullet wound in his shoulder. Fortunately he was able to keep going and made it back to his own lines (in spite of being fired on by mistake from his own comrades!). His diary describes the process whereby a wounded soldier makes it back through the levels of Aid Posts, Field Dressing Stations, Casualty Clearing Stations back to hospital and then on to England.

Part 3 - Special Topics

The Officers

Commanding Officers

Just as there was a high turnover of officers generally, the 1/Wilts also had a high turnover of Commanding Officers. The names of C.O.s during the war - as far as can be gleaned from the War Diary - are given in the table below, together with the approximate length of time in command for each. Only 3 served for more than 100 days. These were Lt. Col. W. S. Brown, who served in total for nearly a year from mid 1915 until he was killed on the Somme battlefield in July 1916. Lt. Col. S. S. Ogilvie acted as C.O. on a number of occasions but his total equalled more than a year. Lt. Col. A. W. Hasted took the battalion over to France, and had two spells in command totalling just under half a year as C.O. The sequence of C.O.s as indicated in the War Diary is given at Appendix F.

C.O.	**Days in Command**	**Approx % of war time in command of battalion**
Austin, Capt. W. M.	10	0.75
Barnard, Capt. Cary	18	1.35
Blake, Maj	74	5.55
Blew, Maj.	? (max 49 days, probably a lot less)	
Brown, Capt. G. D.	52	3.9
Brown, Lt. Col W. S.	342 (approx)	25.66
Cade, Maj. A. G.	5	
Cannon, Maj. H. C.	In command of a segment of the battalion.	
Finlay, Lt. Col. F. D.	27	2.03
Furze, Lt. Col	28 (minimum)	
Frizzell, Maj	3	

Green, Capt. L. B.	? (signs War Diary as o/c 31-05-18)	
Hasted, Lt. Col. A.W.	187	14.03
Hayward, Capt. R. F. J.	3	
Knubley, Capt. R. L.	1	
Ogilvie, S. Lt. Col.	416 (minimum)	31.21
Richardson, Lt. Col. A.	6	
Roche, Maj. T.	79	5.93
Stevens, Maj. G.	3	
Williams, Lt. Col. A. E.	20 (minimum.)	
Wynne, Maj. F. G.	10	

Fig. 5. Time in command (from day mobilisation order received, 4th August 1914 to 11th November 1918)

Officer Casualties

The War Diary, and more particularly the list of 1/Wilts Officer Casualties, enables a picture to be drawn of the officer casualty rates and causes during the war.

A particular problem occurs in defining an officer of the 1/Wilts. During the war many officers from other regiments were drafted in, often on a short term basis. So, even if an officer was seconded to the battalion, and sustained death, wounds, sickness or capture, they are regarded as being with the unit. So also are the members of the R.A.M.C. attached. Based upon this criterion something like around 350 individuals are mentioned in the two sources used. Exact figures are not easy to give since some mis-spelled names may suggest several individuals instead of one. For the (approx) 51 months of the war, and given an average of 26 officers in the battalion, this gives a 'turnover' of around 13.5 times, or once every 3.8 months. Not all of this can be accounted for in casualties: officers left to take up staff or training jobs, or to join other units (where they may have become casualties). Some, of course, were casualties with the battalion. Officers from other units would be drafted in to make up the numbers, only to be replaced themselves when men returned from sick or fresh drafts arrived.

An analysis of the source material indicates that whilst serving with 1/Wilts, the following officer casualties were incurred:

Category	No.	Notes
Killed in Action	70	Includes those missing in action and subsequently deemed to have been killed in action.
Wounded	128	Includes each separate wounding sustained by an officer i.e. an officer wounded more than once has each included in the total.
Sick	115	Includes each separate bout of sickness sustained by an officer. Sickness necessitating officer leaving the unit for treatment. Where several complaints listed in the one period of sickness, the most serious or the one subsequently diagnosed at hospital is given in the analysis later.
Prisoner of War	22	Of these, 2 escaped and 7 were reported to have been wounded prior to capture. Others may also have been wounded.

Fig. 6. Summary of Officer Casualties.

Around 20% of officers serving were likely to be killed in action during their period of duty with the battalion, as against just around 6% who were taken prisoner. Given that some officers were wounded more than once, for every fatality there would be around 1.8 incidents of wounding. Some officers killed in action may have been wounded previously and returned on recovery. The graphs below show casualties by quarter/year. For those killed in action the period marked by the action at Bellewaard (June 1915), the battle of the Somme and the German advances in 1918 were particularly bad.

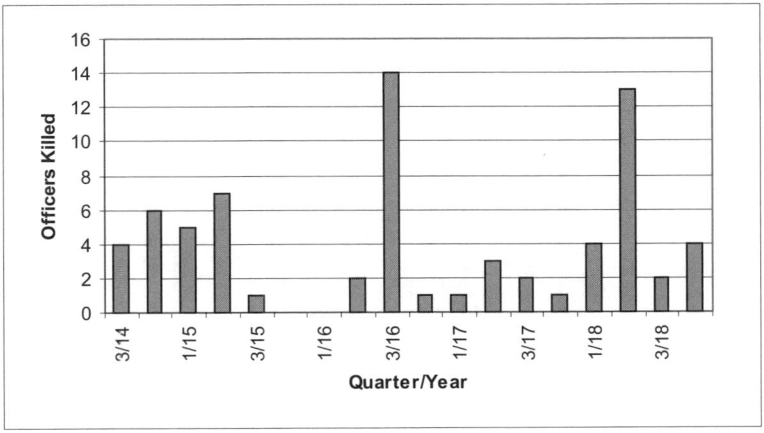

Fig. 7 Officer Fatalities by Quarter and Year
(Quarters 3/14 and 4/18 less than 3 months)

As one would expect, this pattern is reflected in the numbers wounded.

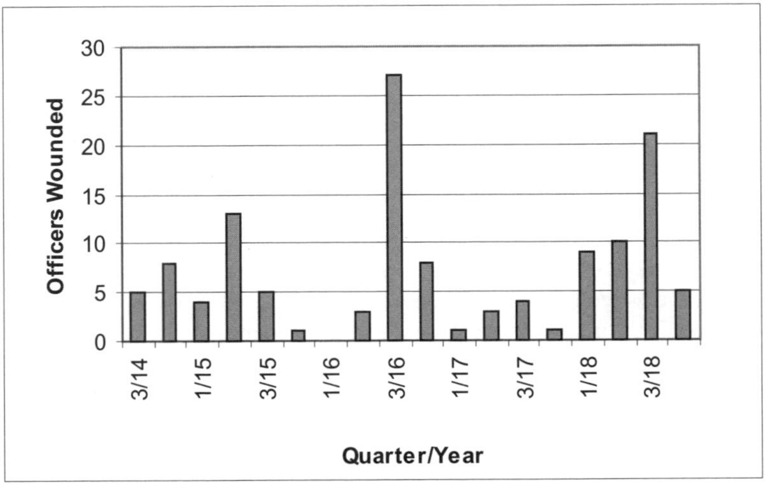

Fig. 8 Officers Wounded by Quarter and Year
(Quarters 3/14 and 4/18 less than 3 months)

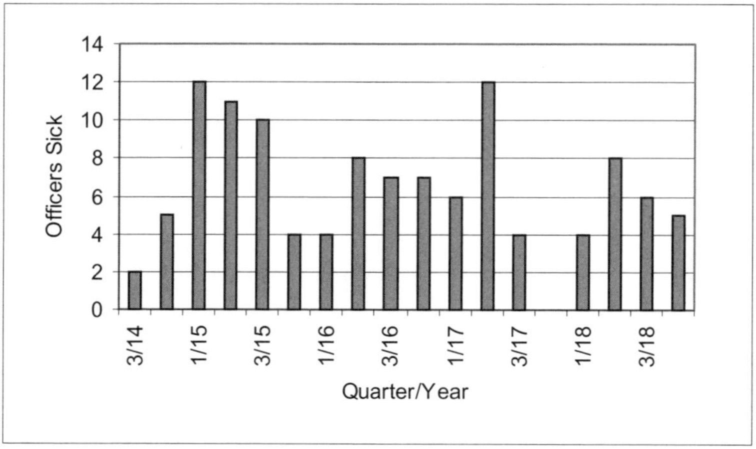

Fig. 9 Officers Absent from Battalion due to Sickness by Quarter and Year
(Quarters 3/14 and 4/18 less than 3 months)

Given the appalling conditions in which they lived, it is perhaps surprising that so many officers did not become sick during their time with the battalion. This is also an impressive reflection on the standards of field hygiene that were maintained in difficult circumstances. There is noticeable tendency for sickness to peak during April-June, with a lower sickness rate during October-December. Perhaps the cold weather made for healthier living. This certainly seems to have been the case with Lt. Swayne:[1]

> We are having a spell of the most piercingly cold weather. Even hardened veterans out since Mons say they have never known it so cold. We are all thankful we are out of the trenches. It is going a bit far when a whisky and soda freezes solid in the glass by your side. I am very fit. I thrive on this weather.

The table below shows the diagnosis made for the various kinds of ailments for each year of the war. Only those bouts of sickness recorded whilst officers were with the 1/Wilts are shown.

---

1 *Letter to parents dated 25th January 1917.*

The figures show that the main problems were Pyrexia (of unknown origin) - 14 cases (to which might be added some of the other conditions such as Trench Fever), and Influenza - 17 cases. One normally associates influenza with the 1918 pandemic, but according to the 1/Wilts records 1915 was a worse year. In neither outbreaks were fatalities recorded. A wide variety of complaints crop up, many of a minor nature. Mention is made of neurasthenia, or 'shell-shock' on six occasions. This diagnosis was made in association with other complaints or following wounding. Quite possibly other labels were given to officers who may have suffered - 'debility' could have been a useful diagnosis. The one case of insomnia is interesting. Given the noise and discomfort it is surprising that the whole army did not suffer from this! M.O.s may also have had their own idiosyncratic way of diagnosis. With the two cases of gonorrhea the officers concerned do not seem to have been required to resign.[2] One returned to duty after treatment at a hospital at Boulogne, although after subsequent illnesses (not V.D.) he was posted to the Devons. The second also rejoined the battalion after treatment, only to be wounded later in action. Diarrhoea was prevalent in 1915, but hardly reported at any other time during the war - although doubtless officers continued to suffer from this complaint.

Complaint	1914	1915	1916	1917	1918	Total
Adenoids		1				1
Appendicitis		1	1			2
Boils			1			1
Bronchial catarrh				1		1
Bronchitis		2	1	3	1	7
Carbuncle					1	1
Catarrhal Jaundice			1			1
Contusion				1		1
Debility		2		1	4	7
Dental Caries			1	1		2
Diarrhoea	1	7				8
Dysentry					1	1

2 *Corrigan (Mud, Blood and Poppycock) points out that the army could require officers to resign if they were unfortunate enough to have contracted the disease, and suggests that few would have been required to do so. The 1/Wilts seems to confirm this.*

Enteritis				2		2
Fracture		1		1		2
Gall stones	1					1
Gastralgia			1			1
Gastritis					1	1
Gonorrhea			1		1	2
Haemorrhoids		1				1
Hernia			2			2
Hypertrophic rhinitis			1			1
Inflammation - naso-pharynx				1		1
Inflammation - stomach		1				1
Influenza	2	7	2	1	5	17
Insomnia	1					1
Lumbago			1			1
Malaria					1	1
Measles		1				1
Mumps			1		1	2
Myalgia		1				1
Nephritis	1					1
Neuritis	1		1			2
Orchitis			1			1
Paralysis			1			1
Periostitis - fibula				1		1
Pneumonia		1				1
Pyrexia		2	4	6	2	14
Rheumatism		4				4
Sick		2				2
Sprain			1	1	2	4
Syncope			1			1
Synovitis				1	1	2
Tonsillitis		2	1			3
Trench Fever		1		1		2

Tuberculosis			1			1
Unfit					1	1
Vision defects			1			1
Not clear					1	1
TOTAL	7	37	26	22	23	115

Fig. 10 Complaints, with numbers sick that required Officers to be treated away from the Battalion.

Fate of Original Officers Landing in France, August 1914

It is generally held that the 'old' British Army ceased to exist after 1st Ypres - i.e. by the end of 1914. The table below illustrates the fate of one group of officers, those embarking with the 1/Wilts in 1914.

Officer	Total days with 1/Wilts	Reason for leaving	Notes
Lt. Col. A. W. Hasted, C.O.	180	Invalided home	Wounded, returned to duty, invalided home, sick.
Major A. S. Barnes	42	Sent home	Ordered to base - reason not given, Sept 1914.
Major T. Roche	98	Killed in Action	Thomas Roche, Major, Died 17/11/14 aged 40. Grave: XI.D.19 Artillery Wood Cemty., Boezinge.
Capt F. W. Stoddart	75	Killed in Action	Frederick William Stoddart, Capt., Died 27/10/14 aged 39. Memorial: Panel 33 and 34 Le Touret Memorial. Chevalier Legion of Honour.
Capt M. C. Richards	208	Invalided home	Transferred to England, Neurasthenia, March 1915. Commanded Cadet Battalion, did not return to front line duties.

Capt W. R. A. Dawes	10	Killed in Action	Walter Richard Aston Dawes, Capt., Died 23/08/14 aged 36. Grave: On the E. side Nouvelles Communal Cemty.
Capt H. R. H. Davies	74	Invalided home	Wounded Nov. 1914. Did not return to active service.
Lieut J. H. M. Mee	125	Invalided home	Wounded Dec. 1914. Did not return to active service.
Lieut P. S. L. Beaver	33	Invalided home	Transfers to 2/Wilts - ends war as Lt. Col.
Lieut W. C. Loder-Symonds	64	POW	Wounded Aug. 1914, P.O.W. Oct. 1914, escaped 1918, killed in aeroplane accident.
Lieut R. H. Broome	237	Invalided home	Wounded April 1915. Further service away from battalion.
Lieut R. G. Browne	28	Died from wounds	Wounded Aug. 1914, returned and wounded again Nov. 1914 (Died of Wounds)
Lieut B. H. Goodhart	318	Invalided home	Invalided back to England, July 1915, Pyrexia.
Lieut T. H. Wand-Tetley	75	POW	Missing, believed prisoner, Nov. 1914.
Lieut K. J. P. Oliphant	75	POW	Missing, believed prisoner, Nov. 1914.
Lieut N. D. Stewart	100	Invalided home	Invalided, sick, Sept. 1914 April 1915, wounded June 1915, then staff appointments.
Lieut E. H. B. Richardson	44	Invalided home	Wounded Oct. 1914. No further active service.
2nd Lieut F. S. Carrington	35	Invalided home	Wounded, rejoins Bttn Feb. 1915, wounded June 1915, staff appointments outside battalion, then sick with Neurasthenia.
2nd Lieut C. C. Morse	211	Invalided home	Wounded March 1915. No further active service.
2nd Lieut H.W. C. Lloyd	75	POW	Wounded slightly, listed as missing P.O.W., escaped 1917.

2nd Lieut E. O. Cruickshank	38	Killed in Action	Eric Onslow Cruickshank, Lt., Died 19/09/14 aged 21. Grave: II.C.13 Vauxbuin French National Cemty.
2nd Lieut H. W. Roseveare	38	Killed in Action	Harold William Roseveare, 2Lt, Died 20/09/14, aged 19. Memorial: La Ferte-Sous-Jouarre.
Capt & Adjutant P. S. Rowan	25	Invalided home	Wounded, August and Nov. 1914, further service as staff officer.
Capt & Q. M., W. I. Cordon	300	Invalided home	Hospitalised May 1915, rejoined Oct. 1915 for 2 months, then Lt. Col. (U.K.).
Lieut P S Power, R.A.M.C., Medical Officer	201	Killed in Action	Pierce Michael Joseph Power, Lt., died 2/3/15 aged 28. Grave: G.31 Kemmel Chateau Military Cemy.

Fig. 11 Original Officer Cadre, August 1914, and subsequent fate.

Of the 25 officers landing in France, 7 (28%) were killed in action or died of wounds, 13 (52%) left because of wounds received or sickness (although some recovered to take up duties outside the battalion), 4 (16%) became prisoners of war, and 1 (4%) was 'sent home' reasons not given. All but the last one left the battalion as casualties (killed, wounded, sick or P.O.W). On average this first group of officers served with the 1/Wilts for 108 days - one being killed within 10 days, and one managing to serve for 318 days. Less than one third would be with the battalion by the first Christmas, and none by the second.

Locations

Although the Great War is often characterised as being 'static' for much of the time - insofar as the front line did not change a great deal - for the soldiers it was certainly one of movement. The 1/Wilts are recorded as occupying just over 200 different locations during the war, and many of these were occupied several times at different periods during the war. The graph below shows the number of occasions the battalion stayed in any one place for the number of days indicated. On just under a hundred occasions their stay was for one day only. The graph drops steeply then onwards, with just over 50 occasions each where the stay was for 2, 3 or 4 days, 4 days being the common tour of duty in trenches, reserve and rest. Only on 11 occasions did they stay for more than a fortnight at any one place, their longest settled period being for 46 days at Outtersteene during Jan-March 1916. The four places where, in cumulative days, they spent the most time were Kemmel (57 days), Locre (54 days), Outtersteene and Ploegsteert Wood (48 days each). A gazetteer of locations is given at Appendix G.

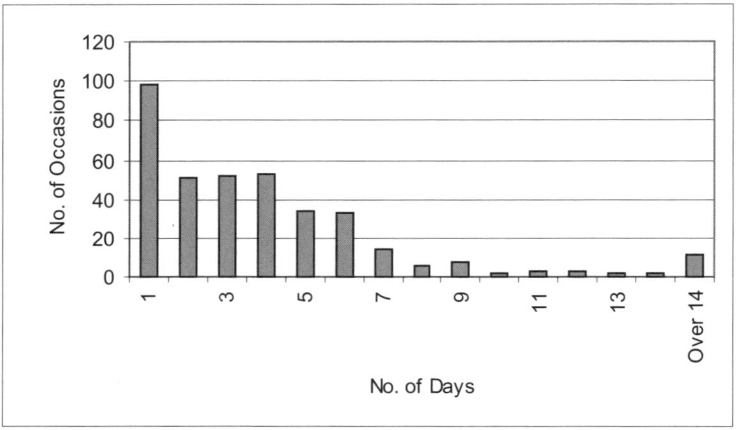

Fig 12 - 1/Wilts Length of Stay in locations from 14-8-14 to 11-11-18

Training

One feature of life on the Western Front which comes out clearly in the War Diary is the extent of training given to both officers and men. The pre-war army had not been trained or equipped for the kind of work it had to do during 1914-1918, but it is a mark of the leadership of the army that it did adapt itself quickly to the new conditions and technology it faced. The history of the 12th Service Battalion York & Lancaster Regiment (City of Sheffield)[3] makes the point well, and it applied equally well to the army as a whole:

> At General Headquarters there was a school for the training of officers for staff appointments; another for advanced teaching of machine gun work to officers and men of machine-gun companies; a third for the benefit of musketry instructors. A Lewis Gun School was established for the instruction of both officers and men. Officers' classes were

3 *By R. A. Sparling, Sheffield, 1920*

> chiefly devoted to organization and tactical subjects, but the men were well trained in the mechanical side of the Lewis Gun, and enabled to realize the properties and limitations of the weapon. There were schools for the teaching of bridging, wireless telegraphy, transport duties, all kinds of field engineering; and then came the Army schools. All the armies, corps, divisions, brigades had their schools, wherein all phases of fighting were taught. The result was that the line units were able to have a continual supply of efficient instructors in the various branches of Army activity. The instructors on their return to the units imparted their knowledge to company commanders and N.C.O.'s, so that every individual in the end was taught the latest development in his particular employment. *The British armies were trained as they fought.* (My italics)

Edmund Blunden[4] rather more cynically suspected that "Probably the underlying cause of the numberless 'schools' in the B.E.F. at this time[5] was as much the desire to give officers and men a rest as to instruct them." Lt. Swayne[6] of the 1/Wilts had a different theory: "I have now gone on a course at XI Corps school. We have 47 officers in the Bn. and they don't know what to do with us, so they sent me here."

The information given on training does reveal the changes in the army's weaponry and tactics. For example, just prior to the Battle of the Somme:

> During this period company and Battn training was continued particular attention was paid to the development of initiative and leadership in section commander and to fire control by the junior N.C.O.s. The advance to the assault and the assault itself were practised, first by single companies and then by the whole Battn, and the part played by specialists such as Lewis Gunners, Signallers and bombers and by carrying and wiring parties, was also demonstrated. In the meantime considerable attention was given to bayonet fighting, and the services of a sergeant major of the Army Gymnasts Staff were utilised for instructing the officers and N.C.O.s. This instruction was then passed on to the men. (21st-27th June 1916) *(War Diary)*

And again, some seven months later:

---

4 *'Undertones of War'.*

5 *Late 1917.*

6 *Letter to parents 15th October 1917.*

> The whole Battn marched to the Div Training Area and practised the capture of two objectives, a front line with its immediate support trenches and a second line. Specialists were given special duties: the snipers to rush out just previous to the assault and fire upon enemy machine guns and snipers, the bombers to push on down CTs and establish blocks, the signallers to establish telephone communication with the position when captured etc. The men were in fighting order and carried tools for the consolidation of the objective. The scheme was carried out twice and the Battn then marched back to Camp (25th January 1917) *(War Diary)*

On 22nd February 1918 two companies practised the assault of strong points and 'other surprise situations'. The other two companies had more traditional fare: a route march and rifle range work. On the following day they swapped training routines. Battalion attack was practiced on 2nd March. Exercises with ball ammunition and rifle grenades took place on 7th March, with night-firing of Very lights. Between 11th-16th March training continued:

> Training was carried out each morning throughout the week 11th - 16th inclusive, particular attention being paid to the musketry training of the Coys. Firing practice upon the range near ACHIET LE PETIT and upon the short ranges in the valley E of LOGEAST WOOD was carried out daily by two Coys, except on the 12th - the day allotted to the Battn for bathing at ACHIET LE PETIT. The latter part of each morning was devoted to Platoon and Coy attack exercises: all ranks, in particular, were trained to act upon surprise orders and officers were on occasion made casualties in to develop the initiative of the NCOs.

In this greater reliance on N.C.O.s the British were following a practice common with the German Army. Attention to the basics of a soldier's trade - musketry - runs throughout. It is also noticeable that training concentrates on the 'attack' throughout the war.

Christmas on Active Service

Unlike the 2/Wilts[7], the first Christmas in the trenches (at Kemmel) was not marked by a truce. Although there was no shelling, snipers were active and the battalion incurred casualties. The War Diary makes no reference to

7 *2/Wilts War Diary records an unofficial truce where both sides met and arranged burial of the dead. A 'Merry Xmas' sign in German was put up in view of the enemy.*

festivities of any kind, although one assumes the men had some sort of treat once they came out of the line.

Christmas 1915 was also spent in the trenches, and this time the Germans made friendly overtures. These were ignored by the 1/Wilts, the whole B.E.F. having been warned that there was to be no repetition of the fraternising that took place during the previous Christmas. The day was spent repairing trenches and receiving visitors - the Corps Commander, no less. The Diary for 1916 shows that New Year's Day was specially celebrated. "Only one fatigue party was required in the morning and there were no parades. The men were given a dinner of pork, Christmas pudding and beer, and at 5p.m. a pierrot party consisting of six officers and one man, entertained a crowded house at the ROMARIN recreation room. At 8p.m. all officers dined together."[8]

December 25th 1916 found the battalion out of the line, and they were able to enjoy the festive season. The Divisional Pierrot Troupe was again called into action on Christmas Eve, with concert and cinema entertainment. On the next day, after Church Parade, Christmas dinner was enjoyed. A party of reinforcements reached the battalion later that day - it is to be hoped that they were able to enjoy the left-overs after their journey, for rail travel to and from the coast was generally slow and uncomfortable.

On 28th December, Lt. R. Swayne reported to his parents:

> We had quite a cheery Xmas, and I actually had a day off fatigues and 2 performances of the pierrots and a Church parade, what a day. We then made a night of it in a tea shop.... up to 1am then up to the trenches breakfast at 6am so we were a poor looking crowd who went up to the trenches on Boxing day. I was the only one who got up in time to fetch the Coy.

Again, in 1917 the battalion was out of trenches for Christmas, but were heavily engaged in fatigues. Christmas Eve was the date for celebrations, with a slap-up dinner and entertainment by our old friends the Pierrots. The following day's account simply records the burying of 400 yards of cable.

The final Christmas, that of 1918, was celebrated in peace, with visits to the men by the Brigade Commander and C.O. Meanwhile a party had returned to

8 *In the army generally officers normally messed by companies due to lack of space and dispersed billets out of the line.*

England to collect the Colours, and these were rejoined with the battalion on New Year's Eve.

Religious Observance

References to Church parades are mentioned at times in the War Diary, although probably more to fill space than as an attempt to keep a proper records. Recording these was not a requirement for the diary. The following Chaplains are recorded:

Rev. L. G. Dickenson - joined 24th October 1915, with two further references in the War Diary for conducting services (31st October 1915 - when he also accompanied the battalion to the trenches - and 2nd July 1916). Rev. Dickenson, it was noted, was from Downton (in Wiltshire).
Capt. C. Beckwith - recorded as joining the battalion 6th July 1917.
Capt. A. M. Robinson - recorded as having been wounded on 2nd September 1917.
Capt. J. S. Barstow - joined 13th September 1917
Capt. D. A. Polhill - joined 1st October 1917, left on 11th October when replaced by Capt. Church.
Capt. W B Church - joined battalion 11th October 1917.
Capt. E E C Iliffe - noted as leaving the battalion to join 47th Labour Corps on 18th March 1919.

In 1917, in a letter home, Lt. Wait says:

> We have sacked our padre and just got a new one. Our other was an awful man, full of gloom with a face as long as from here to Boulogne. He used to creep round the traverses on all fours grasping Woodbines. The men used to call him "Creeping Jesus". Very blasphemous I know, still very funny!! The new on(e) seems a bit cheery & he has a parish near Maidenhead & he used to know Grandfather very well.

In 1914 there are three mentions of Church parade, and nine in 1915. Of these nine, three were specifically described as 'voluntary', and one of these (29th July) had the benefit of the band. Church was cancelled on two occasions in November 1915 - because no men were available due to working parties. In 1916 Church services or parades are mentioned on 19 days, some specifically said to be voluntary. On 23rd April both Church of England and Non-conformist services took place. Of the 8 mentions in 1917, one Church parade (25th March) was taken by the Assistant Chaplain General of the 2nd

Review Concert Party, Christmas 1918

Army. There are only two references for 1918. On 3rd March Church Services were held for 'all denominations' and in the afternoon boxing competitions held - muscular Christianity evidently being the theme of the day.

Sport

The War Diary refers to sports played in the battalion - indeed, at times it reads more like 'the Pink 'Un'. Football is by far the most commonly mentioned sport, and was played at platoon, company, inter-battalion levels and upwards. Generally sports were played in the afternoon after a morning's training. Usually the football would be played by the men, although an officer v. men match is recorded for 9th April 1916, following the distribution of prizes for the main football competition held earlier. The 1/Wilts generally seemed to have played well against other units. In March 1917 the only recorded 'rugger' matches were held. On 1st March the 8/Loyal N. Lancs were the winners, and in a return match on 12th they also a defeated the 1/Wilts. They must have fielded a good side, for the Wiltshires were not without talent. Lt. A. J. S. White[9] writes:

> We played a good deal of soccer and two Rugger matches against the North Lancs Regt. We had one or two good players - Tom Hayward[10] who played for Natal and Middlesex, "Doc" Hughes[11] who became a well-known player for Blackheath of which he has been President for many years, J.T. Wood who has been in the Cheltenham side, and Dick Taylor who had captained Sherbourne.

On 26th March 1916 a novel 'sport' was engaged upon, namely an inter-company ploughing competition using the transport horses and French ploughs. Three older men with agricultural experience were selected for each of the teams. 'D' Company were the winners.

At Lozinghem in September 1917 sport seemed to reach new heights. The War Diary for the period 13-30th records:

> A Div Musketry Comp was held on the 26th preceded by a Bde Comp. This Battn obtained 39 places in the best two shots of the Bde and this

9 *Recollections.*

10 *Capt. R. F. J. Hayward, later to win the V.C.*

11 *Featured in an edition of 'This is Your Life', 1959.*

Battn team of 11 won both the Bde and Div "Falling Tiles" Competition.

The afternoons and evenings were largely devoted to organized recreation, inter platoon and inter company football matches and practising for the 106th Field Coy, RE Sports and Div Sports which took place on the 22nd and 26th respectively. In the latter the Battn won the following places:-

1st Place Pillow Fighting
2nd Place Officers Relay Race
Relay Obstacle Race
Mess Cart turnout
3rd Place Driving Competition.

In the Div Tug of War Comp the Battn after defeating the 8th S Lancs Regt, the Div R E and the 13th Cheshire Regt, was defeated in the semi-final by the RAMC.

The event on 26th was billed as the 25th Divisional Fête, and the 'official' programme for this event exists, having been printed by Harrison and Sons (Printers in Ordinary to His Majesty). Ray Westlake's *'Kitchener's Army'* has an illustration of this.

Boxing occasionally features in the War Diary. Towards the end of March 1916 a competition was held in a barn, and this was held over two days. A little later, on 1st April 1916 Sgt. Lewis of the battalion was easily beaten in a boxing match with a soldier of the 8/Loyal North Lancs. In September of that year the battalion fared rather better, for on the 19th, at Coulon Villers , one man of the four entered for the Brigade Boxing Competition won at his weight. In January 1918 there is further mention of the sport:

> On the majority of the evenings Boxing Matches were held under Coy and Battn arrangements in the 25th Divisional Theatre by the Camp, and in addition a Boxing class was formed and held during the mornings and afternoons under the direction of 2nd Lieut J. J. Riddle.

Lt. Riddle had joined the battalion in October 1917. Perhaps it was due to his efforts that some success was recorded in the entry for 3rd March: "The semi finals and finals of the Div Boxing Competition were fought in the afternoon: Pte Whatley of this Battn defeated his opponent in the welter weight."

Several references are made to cross country running, and sports generally. Also mentioned on several occasions was the need to find suitable space for sports. The War Diary indicates that out of the line there was much emphasis on organised sport as well as practical military training. Since so many men were given the opportunity to play football whilst serving with the forces, it is hardly surprising that attendance at soccer matches reached (according to Simon Inglis)[12] 'unprecedented levels' after the First World War.

Weaponry

The War Diary gives some interesting information on the development and use of weapons during the war. Naturally references to rifles and artillery generally are commonplace. These extracts highlight some of the comments.

Aeroplanes

The War Diary starts its references to aircraft with simply recording their appearance (22th August 1914). Later only multiple numbers deserve mention. Finally, in the latter part of the diary, mention is only made when aircraft directly affect the battalion. On 14th August 1915 enemy aircraft activity prevented the holding of parades whilst at St. Eloi. In October reference is made of attempts (unsuccessful) to down aircraft with machine gun fire. On 7th February 1917 the ineffectiveness of anti-aircraft fire was noted, and later in the year (20th August) the first record of casualties resulting from air bombing was made - one officer and 3 men injured. Lt. Wait[13] recorded an incident involving enemy aircraft:

> A very exciting thing happened the other day - a Boshe (sic) 'plane came over and destroyed one of our observation balloons but before he could get back two of our 'planes forced him to land. He was immediately surrounded by a crowd of "just behind the line" men who with loud cries for vengeance "Remember London" started throwing half bricks and things at him - Disgraceful, isn't it?

A month later (29th December) the men were digging trenches in their rear area camp to provide cover from hostile aircraft. On 13th February 1918 more serious measures were taken, since air attack was clearly becoming a nuisance. Huts were being made bomb proof and Lewis gun positions on a nearby hill were prepared as a counter-measure. On 15th June an enemy aircraft was brought down by rifle fire.

---

12 *'The Football Grounds of England and Wales', Willow Books, 1985.*

13 *Letter to Mother, dated 22nd July 1917.*

Bayonet

Of the 41 references to bayonets, only 3 refer to their actual use in battle. They would routinely be fixed to rifles prior to action. Although not part of the War Diary proper, an attached recommendation for an award is given for Cpl. Bert Vine, who on 23rd August 1916, at Leipzig Salient on the Somme, did "great execution with his rifle and bayonet". The other references are to bayonet exercises forming part of the training schedule out of the line. All three combat references occur in 1914. On 26th October 1914, at Neuve Chapelle, the enemy advanced to within 200 yards of the 1/Wilts, and proceeded to entrench at dusk. Three platoons were used to charge the enemy at bayonet point and drive them out. Later that day, reinforced with elements of other battalions in the brigade, a further attack was made at bayonet point, and the Germans were driven back further. On the following day the battalion's flanks were threatened and close quarter fighting with bayonets was recorded. A bayonet charge was also made that day to try and rescue men captured by the enemy. This, alas, did not prove successful and cost a number of casualties.

A rather more successful encounter with bayonet took place on 17th November at Hooge, when a party of Germans who had penetrated 'D' Company's trenches were evicted with 50 of the enemy killed and many of them wounded.

Bombs/Grenades

The Germans were the first to made effective use of 'bombs' (as hand-thrown grenades were often called). The *Official History* records the date - 27th September 1914. The need for a response was quickly recognised, and the first British 'bombs' were improvised models developed by the Royal Engineers .

Up until the middle of June 1915 the references to bombs in the War Diary were either about being on the receiving end, or about making positions bomb proof. On 12th June 1915 the it appears that the 1/Wilts were making use of these weapons, although unfortunately on that date an accident with a Lyddite[14] grenade killed 2/Lt. Stansfield-Smith and one other man, and wounded 23 others. Four days later they were definitely being used in combat

14 *An high explosive consisting mainly of picric acid, first tested near Lydd in Kent.*

to help clear the enemy from the trenches they had infiltrated. Once the grenades ran out it proved difficult to stem the advance. One indication of the numbers of bombs being employed is given on 30th September 1915, when 125 men were employed in carrying them to a Brigade H.Q. With the introduction of the new weapon came training, as the army began to explore the most effective ways of deploying them. This training features in diary entries from 1915 onwards, and there are innumerable references to bombing used by both sides as a standard means of dealing with their enemies.

An example of their use is described on 19th December 1915:

> 2nd Lieut Cordon and 9 NCO's and men left our trenches to capture a double sentry post in enemy's front trench, which he had reconnoitred on 16th. They entered trench killed two Germans and threw bombs at a counter attack, wounding many of them.

Just over a week later, on the 27th, two new grenade features are mentioned: a rifle grenade and a catapult. The latter device malfunctioned, sending the grenade in the direction opposite to that intended. Two men were wounded, even though lack of faith in the device made them clear the trench before firing. This set back did not seem to deter the men, and the weapon was thought to have been a nuisance to the enemy. Their retaliatory bombardment with mortar and rifle grenades on 5th January 1916 was considered to be aimed at the catapult and mortars in a particular trench.

On 24th April 1916 reference is made to a Bombing Officer (2/Lt Maybrook), who was killed on that date. Enemy mines on 3rd May 1916 destroyed a 'bombing post' within the trench network held by 1/Wilts at La Targette. Clearly bombing was now taken very seriously, and was an integral part of the battalion's defensive and offensive plans. A month later the Germans caused problems at the Birkin Crater post with cylinder stick bombs. On 29th May they were using 'oyster shaped bombs'. "There was a demonstration in the co-operation of Stokes Mortars, Mills Rifle Grenades and Smoke bombs by 3rd Guards Brigade, near BELLE EGLISE which was attended by the C.O. and Bombing Officer." is part of the entry for 11th August 1916, the first mention of smoke bombs.

A curious habit of the Germans was noted on 10th January 1917: "It had become about this time quite a practice with the enemy to throw bombs into his own wire, not only after dark, but in daylight and it was considered that the enemy was engaged in instructing newly arrived drafts."

Occasionally reference is made to new devices: on 3rd May 1917 "Two Rifle Bombing Sections were given instruction in the employment of the No 20 Rifle Grenade" and on 16th February 1918 "Instruction in the use of the Egg Pattern bomb was given to two Coys by the Bombing Officer."

Gas

The Germans first used gas - considered by the British to be in contravention of the agreement of the 1907 Peace Conference at the Hague[15] - in October 1914 and again in January 1915. These early attempts on the Western and Eastern fronts were unsuccessful. Greater impact was achieved against the French at Ypres on 22nd April 1915. 1/Wilts had to wait until 16th June until their exposure to gas was mentioned in the War Diary. The effects were to cause 'temporary inconvenience'. The following January (1916) the men were sent to the Divisional Technical School to be 'gassed'. They were unlucky, as nobody showed up to do the gassing. The next day, 9th January, they marched back to the school and were more fortunate. They were gassed. Even more fortunate was the fact that the 'tubular helmets' they were testing proved up to the task, and they were unaffected.

Gassing by the enemy was not the only hazard from noxious substances. Working in saps, too, was dangerous. On 3 occasions in April 1916 men became casualties through gas underground. On 28th April the men were given 'bomb throwing and gas helmet practice'. This practice was to be needed because on 21st May the battalion received a barrage of lachrymatory shells, resulting in one soldier being affected. More serious was the gas attack on 26th/27th July when the battalion was on the Somme. Casualties here required men to receive treatment out of the line. During August, September and October 1916 there are references to drills and attendance at the Divisional Anti Gas School at Bertrancourt. On 8th November there is the first mention of gas being used by the British, although its planned use on the 1/Wilts brigade front was cancelled at the last moment. Actual use in front of the battalion is first recorded on 11th November at Pont de Nieppe. A bombardment lasting ½hour was directed at the enemy's communication trenches, selected points, and back areas. The commotion caused in the German positions is recorded, with alarms being heard.

---

15 *Section II Article 23 "It is forbidden (a) to employ poison or poisoned arms..." A 'declaration' that "Renounces the use of projectiles, sole object of which is the diffusion of asphyxiating or harmful gases" was "signed by practically all the Powers" (Field Service Pocket Book (1914)).*

The following year, on 10th July at Ypres, the battalion encountered a new and more deadly form - mustard gas. The effects of this gas were noted in some detail in the diary entry for that day, as were the casualties resulting. Later in the month more gas was recorded. During 15th-19th July (Bellewaarde) its use hampered night work on the construction of assembly trenches. A number of gas casualties occurred around Ypres 21st-22nd July 1917. Again at Bellewaarde on 5th August, parts of 1/Wilts had to endure shelling with mustard gas and phosphorus.

In 1918 particular care was being taken over box respirators. On 18th February over the course of 3 hours the Divisional Gas Officer, no less, inspected all of the battalion's appliances. A month later (17th March) the Brigade Gas Officer was entrusted with the same task. For the 4 months following (April-July) there are a further10 references to gassing through enemy shells.

Lewis Gun

Our first mention of this weapon occurs on 7th January 1916, when the diary tells us that a "Lewis Gun Section was formed." Training and parades for the section get several mentions shortly afterwards, but it was not until 17th April that its use in action is described: "The Lewis rifle of A Coy was brought up from the support line and did effective work." An example of the worth of these weapons is given for 5th July 1916, when :

> For immediate award.
> 1st Battn Wiltshire Regt No 19899 Pte Arthur Wheeler
> On the evening of July 5th 1916 at Leipzig Salient during an attack on an enemy trench, Pte Wheeler displayed great courage in bringing up his Lewis rifle, under severe fire, to an exposed flank from which he was able to enfilade the German trench inflicting many casualties on the enemy.
> Recommended by S S Ogilvie Capt. Commanding 1st Wilts Regt.
> Honour awarded. Military Medal.
> 21/7/1916. Major General Commanding 25th Division.

The importance of Lewis guns in defence is indicated in the entry for 9th December 1917, when in the sector at Lagnicourt "The front line was held by a system of posts, there being four posts in each Coy, each with one Lewis Gun."

The menace from enemy aircraft necessitated the use of these weapons in an anti-aircraft role, and on 13th February 1918 the men were engaged upon digging suitable positions for these to be used in defence of their camp.

The value of these weapons was further recognised when the battalion's establishment of them was raised, on 23rd July 1918, from 24 to 36.

Snipers

During 1914 all the references to snipers indicated the problems caused by the enemy. On 3rd November 1915 we get a mention of the battalion using snipers - two Germans being shot at on that day. On the following day Lt. Russell is reported as having done good work with 6 snipers. The, on the 6th November "Our snipers were very successful, knocked over 8 Germans, broke six periscopes and shot down two snipers plates." Capt. Knubley left the battalion on 21st December 1915 to become an instructor at the 25th Division Snipers' School. In the nominal roll of N.C.O.s attached to the entry for 27th January 1916, 6951 L/Cpl Burton, H. is specifically mention as being a sniper. On the next day, 2 men per company plus the snipers spent time reviewing instructions in sniping. Thereafter references to sniping and their casualties, both inflicted and received, are fairly common in the diary.

On 16th May 1916 "one German was sniped and by the use of armour piercing ammunition the enemy was compelled to leave his loophole plates." During the assault on Leipzig Salient during the Battle of the Somme (7th July 1916) a tactic used to silence enemy machine guns is recorded: "Previous to the assault our snipers had been placed in the shell holes in front of their line and fired 30 rounds of steel nosed bullets at the machine guns which had caused so many casualties in the previous attack by D Company. Whether silenced by our snipers or by the bombardment, at any rate the enemy machine gun did not fire during our advance." Later, in November (27th) the G.O.C. Division presented decorations earned by some of the men. Privates Benyon and Whitbread, snipers with the battalion, were given their awards on that occasion. At the end of the year (28th December) it is recorded that Pte. J. R. Wicks[16] was killed by an enemy sniper whilst on wiring duty. The Germans were using a searchlight, based in their support line, to illuminate the scene and to assist their sniping efforts.

---

16 *Buried in London Rifle Brigade Cemetery, Comines-Warneton, Grave II.D.3.*

The importance of snipers is referred to in Lt. White's Recollections. Writing about his experience in the trenches in the winter of 1916-1917 he says:

> The sniper played a very important part in trench warfare. The opposing front-line trenches, which were anything from 100 to 500 yards apart, had been in exactly the same place for two years so both sides had had plenty of time to perfect the arrangements for their snipers. Each of these was ensconced in a heavily protected emplacement which had an opening towards the enemy just large enough for him to see and shoot through. To make him practically invulnerable this opening did not face the trench opposite but was directed diagonally towards a bit of trench further along, the snipers between them covering the whole length of the enemy trench. They were, of course, equipped with telescopic sights with which a marksman was supposed to be able to hit a button at a distance of 400 yards. It can be understood that it would have been suicide to show oneself above the trench in daylight.

Tanks

Curiously there are no direct references to tanks in the War Diary. On 1st September 1918 5 anti-tank guns are listed amongst the material captured from the Germans, and that appears to be the only mention.

In 1916 Lt. Wait wrote home[17] "Isn't (it) splendid, getting Courcelette & Martinpuich. Wish we had Thiepval though - it is rather a hard nut to crack. I should like to see these tanks, I expect I shall soon." A year later, also in a letter[18], he bemoaned the log jam of Captains in the battalion. "I am still doing a Captain's work but I don't know when the other pip is going to roll up. We have so many Captains still on the strength who are doing jobs on Division & Brigade. I am seriously thinking of transferring to the Tanks. Much nicer to get a lift into action than having to walk!"

Trench Mortars

The first mention of a trench mortar was on 3rd April 1915, when a section of the Wiltshire's trench was bombarded by one - but with no damage sustained. On 28th and 29th June the enemy's efforts resulted in casualties. Just over

17 *Letter to his Mother, 23rd September.*

18 *Letter to his Father, 21st September 1917.*

two months later serious damage was done to dugouts in a crater occupied by the battalion. There are several more references to the enemy's use of this weapon until, in December 1915, the 1/Wilts started using trench mortars themselves. Thereafter references to trench mortars and their effects on both sides are made. In May 1916 specific reference is made to a 2 inch mortar being used against the Germans. Evidently this was not appreciated, since they retaliated with a heavy trench mortar - with one being fired at the 1/Wilts every 2 minutes for an hour and a quarter.

Special Divisional Orders attached to the entry for 8th July 1916 refer to the battalion's deeds during their actions on the Somme. During the battle the 1/Wilts were supported by 2 companies of the 3/Worcs., where "The work performed by Lieut Harrison with the Trench Mortar Battery was most effective during the 30 seconds intense bombardment proceeding the attack. His guns were fired no fewer than 100 rounds with greatest accuracy, putting out of action an enemy Machine gun." Lt. D. F. Brown of the 1/Wilts went on a course at the 4th Army Trench Mortar School on 1st August 1916 and on 14th November of that year Lt. J. McDonnell left the Battalion for duty with the 7th Brigade Trench Mortar Battery. All this points to the way in which the B.E.F. was adapting itself to the new weapon and integrating it into its training and tactics. Thereafter the War Diary refers less to trench mortars, presumably since they were now a common feature of the frontline.

Lt. A. J. S. White,[19] following a Trench Mortar course, describes his feelings on the matter of these weapons:

> Though I learnt all about trench mortars I did not relish dropping the shell into the muzzle of the mortar and knowing that if the fuse had not been "crimped" properly it would explode on hitting the striker; and although I believe that accidents were rare it was always a relief to see it emerge safely from the muzzle. Trench mortar officers were never popular, for they had a habit of firing off a few rounds from a certain sector of the trenches and then moving off elsewhere, leaving the occupants of that sector to receive the reprisal rounds from the Germans.

The Stokes mortar gets specific mention from time to time (although it is also referred to as a Stokes gun). It first appears on 8th May 1916. On 27th May a Stokes gun was effective in silencing fire from German aerial torpedoes.

19 *Recollections.*

Thereafter there are references to its routine use at the front. An entry for 5th November 1917 tells us that "The Stokes mortars were usually employed in retaliation for hostile fire, and fired upon enemy front and support lines."

German Weapons

Flammenwerfer

This German device was clearly in use (but not previously encountered by the 1/Wilts) in February 1916. On the 25th of that month a demonstration of the weapon was given under the supervision of the Chemical Adviser for the 2nd Army. The purpose was to show how harmless the liquid fire produced was in reality. This entry alone suggests that the flammenwerfer had already acquired a nasty reputation with the B.E.F. The battalion seemed to have been untroubled by the weapon, although on the last day of 1916 a patrol investigated a possible site where one might be positioned - but drew a blank. It is not until near the end of the war - 13th September 1918 that the War Diary reports: "10.00. Enemy opened a heavy barrage on an behind our line and attacked under cover of flame projectors." Initially the attack was successful but interlopers were ejected fairly readily.

Minen werfer

First specifically mentioned on 6th June 1915, when they were employed against the battalion. They fired 21 shots before being silenced by the British 9.2" guns. Their next mention is on 3rd April 1918, when a large one was reported to be active in bombarding the trench system.

Appendices

Appendix A - The War Diary

The Field Service Pocket Book (1914)[1] states that:

10. War diaries are confidential documents. Their object is:-
(a) To furnish an accurate record of the operations from which the history of the war can subsequently be prepared.
(b) To collect information for future reference with a view to effecting improvements in the organization, training, equipment and administration of the army for war.

11. A diary will be kept in duplicate by:-
Each branch of the staff at general headquarters and at the headquarters of an army, and of all subordinate commands, including garrisons and posts, except intelligence sections of the general staff.
Commanders of permanent and provisional units, detachments from a unit, and base depôts, and the officer i/c A.G.'s office at the base.
Directors and heads of administrative services and departments, and their representatives and officers holding special and permanent appointments, from the first day of mobilization or creation of the particular command or appointment.
The original copy will be forwarded on the last day of each month, unless otherwise ordered, direct to the officer i/c of the A.G.'s office at the base for transmission to the military authorities concerned.
12. In so far as they apply to each case the following points should be recorded:-
(a) All important orders, despatches, instructions, reports and telegrams issued and received, and decisions taken.
(b) Daily situation i.e. arrival at, departure from, or halt at a place; all movements and dispositions on the march, in camp, bivouac, or billets.
(c) All important matters relating to the duties of the staff under their respective headings.
(d) All important matters relating to the administrative services and departments under their respective headings .
(e) Detailed account of all operations, noting connection with other

---

1 *Chapter VIII*

units in the neighbourhood, formations adopted, ranges at which fire was opened, &c. The hour at which important occurrences took place should be entered with exactitude. The state of the weather, conditions of the roads and ground, and general description of the locality should be recorded.

(f) Changes in establishment or strength. As regards casualties, the names and ranks of officers, and the number of other ranks and followers and animals should be noted.

(g) Nature and description of field works constructed or quarters occupied.

(h) Meteorological notes.

(i) Summary of information received and all matters of importance, military or political, which may occur from day to day.

(k)[2] In what respect organizations and regulations have stood the test of war.

13. In all diaries writing should be on one side of the page only.

14. References to appendices, such as orders, reports, telegrams, sketches, statements of evidence of spies and other persons, tabular statements, &c., will be made in the last column.

---

2 *Misprint? sub para (j) missing in my copy.*

Appendix B

Formations including 1/Wilts

Aug '14 - June '15	**Army** – B.E.F **Corps** – II Gen. Sir H. Smith Dorrien
	Division – 3rd (1) Maj. Gen H. Hamilton killed 14.10.14 (2) Maj. Gen. C. Mackenzie invalided 29.10.14 (3) Maj. Gen. F Wing to 22.11.14 (4) Maj. Gen. J. Haldane.
	Brigade – 7th Brig. Gen. F McCracken the Brig. Gen. C Ballard (with 2/Worcs, 2/S.Lancs and 2/Royal Irish Rifles)
June '15 - Oct '15	**Army** – 2nd **Corps** – V Lt. Gen. Sir E. Allanby
	Division and Brigade – as above
May '16	**Army** – 3rd **Corps** –-XVII **Division** as above
	Brigade – 7th Brig. Gen. C Heathcote (from 7th May)
July '16	**Army** – 4th/Reserve Gen. Sir H. Rawlinson
	Corps –-X Lt. Gen. Sir T. Morland then II Lt. Gen. C Jacob
	Division 25th Maj. Gen. E Bainbridge
	Brigade – as above Brig. Gen. C Onslow (from 31st August 1916 with 10/Cheshires, 3/Worcs and 8/Loyal N. Lancs.
Jun-17	**Army** - 2nd Sir H Plumer. **Corps** -II ANZAC Lt. Gen. Sir A. Godley. **Division and Brigade** as above.
Jul-17	**Army** – 5th **Corps** – II **Division and Brigade** as above.
Dec '17 - April '18	**Army** – 3rd Gen. Hon. Sir J Byng. **Corps** – IV Lt. Gen. Sir G. Harper. **Division** as above
	Brigade – 7th Brig. Gen. C Griffin (from 12th Asugust 1917)

26th April '18	**Corps** – XXII **Division** – as above. **Brigade** now consists of 1/Wilts, 10/Cheshire, 4/S. Staffords.
Apr-18	**Army** – 2nd **Corps** – IX Lt. Gen. Sir A. Gordon. **Division and Brigade** as above.
27th May '18	**Division** – 21st
	Brigade as above
21st June '18	**Division** – 21st Maj. Gen. D. Campbell
	Brigade – 110th Brig. Gen. H. Cumming.
July – Nov. 1918	**Army** – 3rd Gen. Hon. Sir J Byng **Corps** – V Lt. Gen C Shute
	Division and Brigade as above

Fig. 13

Appendix C

Route taken by 1/Wilts - 16th August 1914 - 5th September 1914

<table>
<tr><th>Route/Location</th><th>Miles (approx.)</th><th>Notes</th></tr>
<tr><td>Sunday 16th Aug.
France, [Aulnoye]</td><td>0</td><td>Detrained at 7.25p.m., and into billets nearby.</td></tr>
<tr><td>Monday 17th Aug.
France, [Marbaix]</td><td>7½</td><td>Marched with Bde via.Leval.</td></tr>
<tr><td>Tuesday 18th Aug.
France, [Marbaix]</td><td>(6, say)</td><td>Resting in billets, route march.</td></tr>
<tr><td>Wed. 19th Aug.
France, [Marbaix]</td><td>(6, say)</td><td>In billets, route march.</td></tr>
<tr><td>Thursday 20th Aug.
France, [Marbaix]</td><td>10½</td><td>Route march to Avesnes.</td></tr>
<tr><td>Friday 21st Aug.
France, [Feignies]</td><td>19</td><td>Via Dompierre and Mauberge left at 4.10 and arrived 12.30.</td></tr>
<tr><td>Saturday 22nd Aug.
France, [Harmignies]</td><td>16</td><td>Via. Gognies-Bougnies - Asquille. Main part of battalion to Ciply, some Coys outposted at Harmignies.</td></tr>
<tr><td>Sunday 23rd Aug.
France, [Ciply]</td><td></td><td>Ordered to entrench - shelled by the enemy.</td></tr>
<tr><td>Monday 24th Aug.
France, [Ciply]</td><td>15</td><td>Ordered to retire to St. Waas, although Ciply given as location in War Diary.</td></tr>
<tr><td>Tuesday 25th Aug.
France, [Coudry]</td><td>23½</td><td>Via. Gommignies - Solesmes. Actions fought at both locations.</td></tr>
<tr><td>Wed. 26th Aug.
France, [Coudry]</td><td rowspan="2">34</td><td>When retirement was ordered Wilts fell back to Beaurevoir via Elincourt and Malincourt.</td></tr>
<tr><td>Thursday 27th Aug.
France, [Ham]</td><td>At 2 a.m. retired to Hagicourt where halted for a few hours. Then to Vermand, halted 5 hours. Finally to Ham.</td></tr>
</table>

Friday 28th Aug. France, [Tarlefesse]	8½	
Saturday 29th Aug. France, [Salency]	4½	
Sunday 30th Aug. France, [Vic sur Aisne]	17	Crossed River Oise near Varennes.
Monday 31st Aug. France, [Coyolles]	13	
Tuesday 1st Sept. France, [Villiers St Genest]	8½	7.30 a.m. retired towards Levignen, where turned back to cover retreat. Then on to Villiers St. Genest.
Wednesday 2nd Sept. France, [Marcilly]	7	Battalion right at Barcy.
Thursday 3rd Sept. France, [Sancy]	11	4.45a.m. withdrew from outpost position, retired on Pringy. Ordered to provide flank guard at Barcy. Reached Meaux at 12 noon, where held position whilst bridge destroyed. Reached Sancy at 6p.m.
Friday 4th Sept. France, [Châtres]	13	Left Sancy about 11p.m.
Saturday 5th Sept. France, [Châtres]		
TOTAL distance	220 miles	Between 17th August and 4th September (19 days) the battalion averaged nearly 12 miles a day during which it fought, guarded and performed other duties.

Fig. 14

Appendix D

Shot at Dawn - The Case of Pte. Tanner

One of the earliest examples of a soldier being shot for desertion occurred in the 1/Wilts in October 1914. The details are recorded in a piece written by Julian Putkowski which can be found on the website:

http://www.shotatdawn.org.uk/tanner.htm.

As recorded on the website, Pte Tanner became detached from a party of comrades on the night of 18th October in the village of Haplegarde. He was returning to duty after having been hospitalised for dysentry. He slept in the village, and on the following morning was detected by an officer of the 2/S. Lancs. He was wearing army boots, but had otherwise changed into civilian clothes and had discarded his rifle. On being arrested he led his guards to the place where he had hidden his uniform and rifle. A Field Court Martial at which Capt. Mosley of 1/Wilts sat tried him on 23 October. The F.C.M. sentenced him to death.

The account on the website makes a point that those who judged Tanner were not impartial, and that no account was made of his previous record.

The account also lists 11 officers who were captured by the Germans between 23rd and 27th October - 6 of whom were with the 1/Wilts[1]. It calculates this as being one third of the battalion's officers. The account recognises that some of the officers were wounded when captured, but says that others "effectively surrendered". "So much for the sake of example" is its conclusion.

Historians more competent than this writer have debunked many of the contentious views expressed in "Shot at Dawn"[2]. The implication of interest

---

1 *These figures do not quite tally with the Officer Casualty List. Lt Rose was captured after the period (31st October 1914). In addition Lts W.C. Loder-Symonds and M.K. Watson were taken prisoner during the period. Of the 7 men captured (all except perhaps 1 on 27th October 1914), 2 subsequently escaped from Germany, and 2 were recorded as being wounded (others might have been).*

2 *e.g. 'Capital Courts-Martial during the Great War' by John Peaty, an essay in 'Look to Your Front' and 'Blindfold and Alone' (Cathryn Corns & John Hughes-Wilson).*

here is that the 1/Wilts officers who were captured were no better than Pte. Tanner. The War Diary refutes this suggestion. It is clear that the battalion, with its outflanked units, were outnumbered by the enemy, and they held their line in the face of every possible likelihood of annihilation. Those in the front line- officers and men - were deprived of sleep due to the constant night attacks and use of fresh soldiers by the enemy. Capture of officers by the enemy was relatively rare occurrence in the 1/Wilts. Throughout the war only 22 suffered this fate, as opposed to some 77 officer fatalities. Apart from one wounded officer captured in 1916 one has to wait until the German onslaught of 1918 for others to be captured. On release officers were required to account for the circumstances of their capture, it being quite acceptable to surrender to the enemy once deprived of effective means of resistance.

The incident is mentioned in J.F. Lucy's *'There's a Devil in the Drum'*. Lucy, then an N.C.O. in the 2/Royal Irish Rifles, doubted whether such actions had the intended effect on the rank and file generally, and says that the executions 'disgusted the fighting men'.

Appendix E

Analysis of N.C.O. Roll, January 1916, Outtersteene Camp

Rank	Company			
	A	B	C	D
Sergeant Major			1	
Company Sergeant Major	1	1	1	1
Quarter Master Sergeant			1	
Company Quarter Master Sergeant	2	2	1	
Sergeant	9	9	11	11
Lance Sergeant	2	2	4	
Corporal	10 (1 at div. school)	8	9	10
Lance Corporal	27	17	17	23
TOTAL	51	39	45	45
Grand Total	140			

Fig. 15

Specialisms / Specific duties mentioned

A Coy:
1 Sgt Machine Gun
1 Provost Sgt
1 Sgt. Orderly Room Clerk
1 Cpl Signaller
1 L/Cpl Post Room Cpl.
1 L/Cpl Coy Orderly
1 L/Cpl Regimental Tailor

1 L/Cpl C.O.'s orderly
1 L/Cpl Machine Gun
1 L/Cpl Transport
1 L/Cpl Pioneers
1 L/Cpl Officers' Cook
1 L/Cpl Signaller
B Coy
None
C Coy
1 Sgt. Armourer
1 Sgt. Shoemaker
D Coy
1 Sgt. Master Cook
1 Sgt. Signaller
1 Cpl. Transport
1 Cpl. N.C.O.'s School of Instruction
2 L/Cpl. Machine Gun section
1 L/Cpl. Grenadiers
2 L/Cpl Signallers
2 L/Cpl Orderlies
1 L/Cpl Sniper

Appendix F

Sequence of Commanding Officers

Period From - To	Officer	Notes
04-08-14 to 20-09-14	Lt. Col. A. W. Hasted	(C.O. at start of war, wounded)
20-09-14 to 07-12-14	Maj. T. Roche	Killed in post
07-12-14 to 24-04-15	Lt. Col. A. W. Hasted	(returns following wound, leaves due to sickness)
24-04-15 to 11-05-15	Capt. Cary Barnard	(vice Lt. Col. Hasted, sick)
11-05-15 to 23-07-15	Major Blake	(later temp Lt. Col.)
23-07-15 to 12-04-16	Lt. Col. W.S. Brown	Left to take temp. command of Bde)
12-04-16 to ?before 30-04-16	Capt. T. M. H. Kincaid Smith	(temp command mentioned on that date)
? before 30-04-16 to 05-07-16	Lt. Col. W. S. Brown	(killed, in post)
05-07-16 to ? 05-07-16	Capt. R. L. Knubley	(until arrival of Capt. Ogilvie)
05-07-16 to 14-07-16	Capt. S. Ogilvie	
14-07-16 to 16-07-16	Maj. G. Stevens	(from and back to Royal Fusiliers)
16-07-16 to 21-07-16	Lt. Col. A. Richardson	(leaves to take command of 8/S. Lancs)
21-07-16 to 5-09-16	Capt. S. Ogilvie	
05-09-16 to 07-09-16	Maj. Frizzell	(from 1/Berks)
07-09-16 to 03-10-16	Lt. Col. F. D. Finlay	(leaves due to sickness (from 2/Wilts))
03-10-16 to 12-10-16	Capt W. M. Austin	(vice Lt. Col Finlay, sick)
12-10-16 to ?after end Oct.16	Lt. Col. A. E. Williams	(late Worcs. Regt.)

?before end Dec. 16 to 06-07-17	Maj . S. Ogilvie	(resumes command after having been wounded, goes on leave)
06-07-17	Capt. G. D. Brown	(vice Maj. Ogilvie, leave)
31-07-17 to 13-10-17	Lt. Col S. Ogilvie	(date returned not clear, leaves on temp. command 7 Inf. Bde)
13-10-17 to before 30-11-17	Maj. Blew	
before 30-11-17 to 24-01-18	Lt. Col S. Ogilvie	(date returned not clear, leaves on temp. command Bde)
24-01-18 to 26-01-18	Capt. R .F. J. Haywood	temp whilst Col. Ogilvie i/c Bde
26-01-18 to 20-02-18	Maj. G. D. Brown	(rejoins battalion from 4/S. Staffs)
20-02-18 to 01-03-18	Maj. F. G. Wynne	(from 8/N. Lancs - killed N. of River Lys)
01-03-18 to 10-04-18	Lt. Col S. Ogilvie	(missing N of R Lys)
10-04-18 to 22-04-18	No C.O. mentioned	Bttn appears disorganised due to German advance
22-04-18 to 26-04-18	Maj. A. G. Cade	(killed, in post)
27-04-18 to ?30-04-18	Maj. H. C. Cannon	(Was 2 i/c, from Queen's Regt.)
?30-04-18 to 27-05-18	Lt. Col. Furze	(wounded and taken prisoner). Exact date of arrival unclear -signs War diary on 30 April, but entry for 4th May 1918 states took over on that date)
27-05-18 to 19-06-18	Maj. Cannon and Capt Parkes lead 2 separate detachments of 1/Wilts in retirement. No overall C.O. mentioned	Split due to German advance

31-05-18	Capt. L.B. Green signs War Diary as C.O. 1/Wilts	1/Wilts still in separate detachments at this stage
19-06-18 to ?before 30-06-18	Maj. J. T. Bridges	From Worcs Regt.
?30-06-18	Maj. H. C. Cannon	Signs War Diary as C.O.
07-07-18 to 13-08-18	Lt. Col G. B. C. Ward	(from S Wales Borderers, recFrom S. Wales Borderers.
13-08-18 to 29-08-18	Maj. Muirhead	Attached from 1st Lancers, leaves, wounded
29-08-18 to ?31-08-18	Maj. G. T. Parkes	vice Maj. Muirhead wounded
?31-08-18 to 13-10-18	Lt. Col G. B. C. Ward	(signs War Diary on 31-08, assumes command of 110th Inf. Bde.)
13-10-18 to 11-11-18	Maj. G. T. Parkes	vice Lt. Col Ward, commanding Bde and on leave
11-11-18 to 14-11-18	Lt. Col G. B. C. Ward	Assumes command of 110th Inf Bde
14-11-18 to 07-12-18	Maj. G. T. Parkes	vice Lt. Col Ward, commanding Bde
07-12-18 to 21-12-18	Lt. Col G. B. C. Ward	Goes on leave England
21-12-18 to 05-01-19	Maj. G. T. Parkes	
05-01-19 to 10-02-19	Lt. Col G. B. C. Ward	Returns from leave, assumes command110th Inf. Bde
10-02-19 to ?29-03-19	Maj. G. T. Parkes	Proceeds to Corps Concentration Camp for demobilisation
?29-03-19 to 29-05-19	Lt. Col G. B. C. Ward	1/Wilts embark for home

Appendix G

Gazetteer of Places occupied by 1/Wilts During the Great War

Location	Total Days stayed	Position
Abbeville	1	16km SE of Somme Estuary. Detrained here after leaving the area of the Aisne and en route to Flanders 1914.
Abeele (Belgium)	13	6km SW of Poperinge. Out of line, July and October 1915, rest September 1917.
Acheux Wood	6	11 km NW of Albert. Training, July 1918.
Achiet le Grand	39	5km NW of Bapaume. Training, working parties February-March 1918. Here when the German offensive started.
Achiet le Petit	1	7km WNW of Bapaume. Stopping point during German advance, 1918.
Acq	7	2km W of Mont St. Eloi. Rest, April, May 1916.
Albert	1	Bivouacked by lake east of Albert during Battle of Somme, July 1916.
Amerval	2	4.5km N of Le Cateau. In pursuit of enemy, advance November 1918.
Arcis le Ponsart	14	23km W of Reims. The first camp used on arriving in the Champagne area prior to the Battle of the Aisne, May 1918
Augy	1	Just SW of Braine. Stopping place during move to Flanders, 1914.
Aulnoye	3	(Aulnoye-Aymeries) 28km S of Mons. Detrained prior to Battle of Mons, and in pursuit of enemy, advance November 1918.
Aveluy Wood	1	About 5km N. of Albert. Last stop before Battle of Somme, July, 1916.
Bailleul	6	11km NW of Armentieres. Training October 1915.
Barastre	4	6km SE of Bapaume. Rest, December 1917.

Barly	3	18 km NE of Doullens. Training etc. en route for the Somme battlefield, June 1916.
Beaulencourt	6	3.5km SSE Bapaume. Advance, August '18.
Beau Metz	1	9km ENE of Bapaume. Stopping place.
Beaumont Hamel	3	9km N of Albert. Start of advance Aug. 1918.
Beaunay	1	19km SSW of Épernay. occupied during German advance, May 1918.
Beauval	2	5km S of Doullens. Resting after Battle of Somme, July 1916.
Bellewaarde	11	4.5km E of Ypres. Trenches, July and August 1917.
Berlaimont	3	15km SW of Maubeuge. In pursuit of the enemy, advance November 1918. Here when the armistice came into effect.
Bethune	1	15km NW of Arras. Staging post to the line, Givinchy, November 1917.
Bezu le Guery	1	13km WSW of Chateau Thierry. 1st stop after crossing River Marne on advance to River Aisne, 1914.
Bissezeele	4	14km S of Dunkirk, on D928. Rest, training on way to Champagne area, May 1918.
Bois de Coutron	2	Approx 13 km SW of Reims. Holding position against German advance, June 1918.
Bois du Warnimont	2	In area of Somme battlefield. Training.
Bois d'Eclisse	7	Near Bois de Coutron. Holding position against German advance, June 1918.
Bouzincourt	8	5km NW of Albert. Rest and training, August and September 1916
Braine	10	16km ESE Soissons, on River Vesle. Base for actions further N. at Vailly, 1914.
Branscourt	1	14km WNW of Reims. Retirement during German advance, May 1918.
Burbure	1	12km W of Bethune, 3km S. of Lillers. In billets, November 1917.

Bus les Artois	6	14km NNW of Albert. Training etc. August 1916
Busseboom (Belgium)	19	3km SE of Poperinge. Rest etc. July and September 1915.
Bussiques (Bussieres)	1	18km SW of Chateau Thierry. Stopping place on advance to River Aisne, 1914.
Caistre	1	6km NE of Hazebrouck. Staging post on way to I Corps area, September 1917.
Caudry	2	8km W of Le Cateau, 8km SSW of Solesmes. Just off N42. Held the centre of the line here during Battle of Le Cateau.
Caullery	12	13km SE of Cambrai. Reorganisation and training, October 1918.
Chantereine Fram	6	Near Beaunay. Occupied June 1918 after Battle of the Aisne, just before being relieved by an Italian unit.
Châtres	2	22km NNE Melun. The southernmost point reached during the 1914 Retreat.
Chelers	12	21km WNW of Arras. Rest, training, refitting etc. June 1916.
Ciply	2	nr Mons. Position held (in reserve) during Battle of Mons
Clapham Junction	2	Just E of Ypres. In the front line, August 1917.
Coulommiers	1	22km SE of Meaux. Billeted at Paper Mill during advance to River Aisne, 1914.
Coulon Villers	13	13.5km ENE of Abbeville. Training, September 1916.
Coyolles	1	26 km SW of Soissons. Stopping place on retreat from Mons, 1914.
Crucifix Corner (1)	1	3km NNE of Albert. This was the entrance to a communication trench used to gain access to the trench system around Ovillers
Crucifix Corner (2)	3	Nr. Neuve Eglise. In trenches, April 1918.
Dammard	1	18km NW of Chateau Thierry. On route to advance to River Aisne, 1914.

Delettes	12	15km SSW of St. Omer. Training June/July and November/December 1917.
De Seule Camp	17	6km ESE Bailleul. Rest, training and working parties, January 1917.
Destremont Farm	4	Near Eaucourt and Beaumont Hamel. August 1918. Occupied during advance.
Dickebush or Dickebusche (Belgium).	37	Now Dikkebus. 5km SW of Ypres. Stayed at various times either in trenches or for periods of rest.
Dominion Camp	3	E of Busseboom. Training, August 1917.
Donnets Post	4	near Thiepval. October 1916.
Doulieu (le Doulieu)	1	6km S of Bailleul. Marched to billets here after Battle of La Bassée, 1914.
Douve (sector)	3	Just N of Ploegsteert Wood. In trenches April 1918.
Elzenwalle	32	5km SW of Ypres, nr Dikkebus. In trenches.
Englebelmer & Wood	28	7.5km NNW of Albert. In rotation support and trenches in these positions during July/August 1918.
Englefontaine	1	27km E of Cambrai, of W edge of Forêt de Mormal. In pursuit of the enemy, Nov. '18.
Equancourt	3	15km SE of Bapaume. Attacked enemy during advance September 1918.
Esquerdes	13	8km SW St. Omer. Training, May 1917.
Etricourt	3	11km SE of Bapaume. Passed during advance September 1918.
Faverol (Faverolles)	1	16km WSW of Reims. Retired to positions here during German advance, May 1918.
Favreuil	31	1.5 km N of Bapaume. Rest, training etc. December 1917 and January/February 1918.
Feignies	1	4km NW Maubeuge. During march N. to Mons, August 1914.
Forceville	3	10km NW of Albert. Resting after Battle of Somme, July 1916.

Fremicourt	3	3km E of Bapaume. Attempted stemming of German advance, March 1918. Capt. Hayward won the V.C. here.
Gezaincourt	6	2km SW of Doullens. Rest etc. after Somme battle, October 1916.
Givenchy	13	8km E of Bethune. In support and trenches October/November 1917.
Givenchy (in line near)	18	As above.
Gommecourt	1	15km N of Albert. Stopped off during German advance March 1918.
Gorre	16	On NE outskirts of Bethune. Reserve and working parties, October/November 1917.
Gouzeaucourt	3	16km SSW of Cambrai. Attacked enemy positions during advance September 1918.
Grand Rozoy	3	16km S of Soissons. Stayed during advance to River Aisne, and later during move to Flanders, 1914.
Guyencourt	1	18km NW of Reims. Moved up to meet German attack, May 1918.
Half Way House	2	E of Ypres near Westhoek. August 1917. Stopping points.
Halifax Camp	3	On Ouderdom-Vlamertinghe road, a hutted camp. August 1917, baths and rest.
Halley les Pernois	10	16km NNW of Amiens. Training etc. prior to move to Somme battlefield, June 1916.
Ham	1	On outskirts of Noyon. Stopping place on retreat from Mons.
Hamel	6	7km N of Albert. In trenches end July 1916.
Haplegarde	2	1.5km N of La Bassée. Not shown on modern map. Scene of fierce fighting during Battle of La Bassée, 1914.
Hardinval	1	4km W of Doullens. Stopping place, September 1916.
Harmignies	1	8km SE of Mons. Occupied prior to Battle of Mons, August 1914.

Hedauville	5	7.5km NW of Albert. Training and rest after action at Leipzig Salient, August 1916.
Heudicourt	10	18km SE of Bapaume.Attacked by Germans during the British advance, September 1918.
Hindenburgh Line	3	In the War Diary, a position just E. of the Canal around 14km S. of Cambrai
Hinges	1	5km NNW of Bethune. Billeted here on way to Battle of La Bassée.
Hooge (Belgium)	47	5km E of Ypres. Occupied trenches during Nov. 1914 and various periods during 1915. Particular action 25 September 1915.
Hurtebise Farm	2	Near Warlencourt. Advance, October 1918.
Kemmel (Belgium)	57	9km SSW of Ypres. In trenches at various periods during 1914 and 1915.
La Bassee	3	12km E of Bethune. Brigade support, November 1917.
La Boisselle	1	4km NE of Albert. During Battle of Somme, July 1916.
La Brique (Belgium)	5	In trenches August 1915.
La Clyte	6	Now De Klijte , 8km SW of Ypres, between Locre and Dickebush. In billets, March 1915, trenches April/May 1918.
La Couture	4	6km NNE Bethune. Opening stages of Battle of La Bassée, in billets after battle
La Targette	18	7.5km NNW of Arras. In trenches April May 11915. Mining.
La Triquerie	2	7km N of Abbeville. Billeted at La Triquerie Chateau on way to Flanders, 1914.
Lagnicourt	23	9km NE of Bapaume. In trenches December 1917, January/February 1918.
Le Bizet (Belgium)	20	Now N suburb of Armentieres. In support, trainingwinter 1916/17
Le Charnois (Le Charnoy)	1	9km WNW Coulommiers. Stopping place on advance to River Aisne, 1914.

Le Meux	1	8km SW of Compiegne. Entrained here for Abbeville en route to Flanders, 1914.
Le Parc	1	In Forêt de Nieppe 7km S of Hazebrouck. In transit.
La Tete Noir	1	3km W of Barlaimont, on E edge of Forêt de Mormal. In oursuit of enemy, November 1918.
Le Touquet	36	On River Lys, 5km NE Armentieres. In trenches November, December 1916 and April 1917.
Lealvillers	2	12km NW of Albert. Rest after action at Leipzig Salient, September 1916.
Leipzig Salient	14	1km S of Thiepval. In battle and manning trenches during Battle of Somme, July to September 1916.
Ligny le Grand	4	3m E of Neuve Chapelle. Scene of further action during Battle of La Bassée.
Lisbourg	3	25km S. of St. Omer. Stopping point on way to join 3rd Army, December 1917.
Locre (Belgium)	54	Now Loker, near Kemmel. Stayed to rest and absorb reinforcements after Battle of La Bassée and during 1915.
Locre Chateau	1	On Bailleul Rd. Retiring before German advance during Battle of the Lys, April 1918.
Lozinghem	21	11km W of Bethune. Rest and training, September 1917.
Lys, N. of River	3	In sector near Ploegsteert Wood, April 1918.
Mailly Wood	8	Just SW of Mailly-Maillet, 10km N of Albert. Training etc. August 1916.
Marbaix	4	8km S of Aulnoye. In billets prior to moving on to the Mons area Aug. 1914
Marcilly	1	9 km N of Meaux. Stopping place on retreat from Mons, 1914.
Menin Road	3	West of Hooge. In trenches, action on 16th June, 1915.
Mille-Bosc	11	12km SE of le Tréport. Joined 110th Brigade and 21st Division, rest, reorganisation training etc. June 1918.

Mont des Cats	17	7km SSW of Poperinge. Training etc., February March 1917.
Mont St Eloy	5	7.5km NW of Arras. In huts, April 1916.
Montrelet	4	21km N. of Amiens. Occupied during German advance, March 1918.
Mouquet Farm	3	(Mouquft in trans) 1.5km E of Thiepval. In support during attack on Regina Trench, October 1916.
Nedonchelles (Nedonchel)	1	18km W of Bethune. In transit, June 1917.
Neuve Chapelle	6	12km NE of Bethune. Scene of desperate action during Battle of La Bassée. Also on removal from area of German advance April 1918.
Neuve Eglise	24	Also known as Nieuwkerke, 6km E Bailleul. Various stays in support and providing working parties, 1917. Stayed for part of time at 'Bulford Camp' in the vicinity.
Noote Boom	9	SW of Bailleul. Training, rest etc. March 1917.
Nord Helf	1	1.5km N. of Merris, 9 km E of Hazebrouck. Billeted here after Battle of La Bassée.
Noroy	1	18km SSW of Soissons. On River Ourq. Stopping place on move to Flanders, 1914.
Ouderdon (Belgium)	6	7.5km WSW of Ypres. Out of line, August 1915 and on way to line, 1918.
Outtersteene	48	4.5km SW Bailleul. Training February to March 1916, March 1917.
Ovillers	5	6km NNE of Le Cateau. Attacked enemy positions and later in billets, October 1918.
Papot	31	In vicinity of Ploegsteert Wood.Training and in reserve during various periods late 1915 and late 1916.
Péas	2	3km NE Sézanne, 36km SSW of Épernay. Rest etc. after Battle of the Aisne, June 1918.
Penin	1	12km ESE of St. Pol. Transit during move to Somme battlefield June 1916.

Pernes	1	16km WSW of Bethune. Arrived by motor transport and went into billets prior to Battle of La Bassée.
Piggeries	20	Near Ploegsteert. Rest etc. November 1915.
Ploegsteert	11	4.5km N of Armentieres. In trenches November 1916.
Ploegsteert Wood	48	Just N of Ploegsteert. In trenches late 1915 early 1916. Rest and in trenches, April 1918.
Poix du Nord	5	Just to the W of Engelfontaine (see above). In pursiut of the enemy October/November 1918.
Pont de Nieppe	32	? Bridge over River Lys at Armentieres on road to Nieppe, 3km NW of bridge. In trenches or in reserve late '16 and early '17.
Pont Logy (Pt. Logis)	1	1km W of Neuve Chappelle. Position taken at later stage of Battle of La Bassée.
Poperinghe (N)	4	8km W of Ypres. April '18 - rest after 2nd Battle of Kemmel.
Pradelles	2	4.5km E Hazebrouck. March 1917.
Pronville	2	13km NE Bapaume. Working parties, February 1918.
Prouilly	3	13km WNW of Reims. Training, May 1918.
Puchevillers	4	12km SSE of Doullens. Training August 1916. Occupied during German advance March 1918.
Pylones (Bethune-Arras Rd.)	21	Just N. of Neuville St. Vaast, 3km WSW of Vimy. In trenches May 1916. Longest continuous occupation of trench position.
Raincheval	23	16km NW of Albert. Occupied prior to action at Thiepval, September 1916. Training, July 1918.
Ravelsberg	5	nr Bailleul (E). Rest and working parties May and June 1917.
Ravelsberg Hill	6	as above.
Regnauville	1	27km NNE of Abbeville, 10 km S of Hesdin. Stopping place on march to pick up transport for move into Flanders, 1914.
Reninghelst	11	9km WSW of Ypres. Rest and training, July 1917. In trenches just to the E May 1918.

Riveld	4	3km NE of Cassel, 11 km N of Hazebrouck. Training, August 1917.
Robecq	2	10km NNW of Bethune. Stopping point on march S March 1916.
Romarin	7	5km NW of Armentieres, 2km WSW of Ploegsteert. In trenches February, 1917.
Rouen	1	Port of entry into France in 1914
Rubempre	1	19km W of Albert. Stopping point after Somme battle, October, 1916.
St Aignan	1	Just N of Rouen. Camped here on arriving in France August 1914
St Eloi	13	5km S of Ypres. In trenches various times during 1915.
St. Jean	9	Near St. Eloi. In trenches August 1915.
St Venant	1	12km NW of Bethune. In transit, June 1917.
Sailly-Saissisel	2	9km SSE of Bapaume. Advance, September 1918.
Saintines	1	12km S of Compiegne. Stopping place on move to Flanders, 1914.
Salency	1	4km E of Noyon. Stopping place on retreat from Mons, 1914.
Sancy	1	12km SSE Meaux. Stopping place on retreat from Mons, after crossing River Marne.
Sarton	3	7km SE of Doullens. Training etc. August 1916.
Savy	2	? Savy-Berlette, midway between St. Pol and Arras. On route N to trenches La Targette, April 1916.
Scherpenberg (Belgium)	2	Just NW of Kemmel. In billets, Novermber 1914.
Sercus	9	6km WSW Hazebrouck. Training various dates 1917.
Sercy (Sarcy)	1	16km WSW of Reims. Retirement during German advance, May 1918. From a position just E of here, by River Ardre, battalion divided into 2 forces, June 1918.

Sorel le Grand	4	17km SE of Bapaume. Advance, September 1918.
Steenacker	4	Near Poperinghe. Rest and reorganisation following German advance during 2nd Battle of Kemmel, April 1918.
Steenbecque	2	7km SSW of Hazebrouck. In transit July,1917.
Steentje	5	Just S of Bailleul. Training, working parties, April 1917.
Steenvorde	10	10km WSW of Poperinge. Rest and training, August 1917. Stopping place en route for Chemin des Dames area May 1918.
Strazeele	5	6 m. E of Hazebrouck on Bailleul road. Training, April-May 1917.
Stuff Redoubt	6	Part of German defences, N. of Thiepval. In trenches October 1916.
Tannay	2	11km SSW of Hazebrouck. Stage on march to I Corps area September 1917.
Tarlepesse (Tarlefesse)	1	5km NE of Noyon. Stopping place on retreat from Mons, 1914.
Ternas	24	25km W of Arras, 6km SE of St. Pol. Training, March 1916. Ploughing contest took place here
Thiepval	9	7km NNW of Albert. Scene of action during Battle of Somme, October 1916.
Tidworth	10	On E edge of Salisbury Plain. Based here when war declared.
Usna Hill	5	1 km W of La Boisselle, 2.5 km NE of Albert. Rest after action at Leipzig Salient, July 1916.
Vailly	8	15km ENE of Soissons. Position held on N. bank of River Aisne during the period of initial trench warfare at end of advance to the Aisne, 1914.
Valhuon	5	21km WSW of Bethune, on D916. Training March 1916.
Varennes	3	9kn NW of Albert. On way to Somme battlefield, July 1916.

Vaulx-Vraucourt		6km NE Bapaume (referred to as Vaulx in War Diary). Brigade reserve, working parties, December 1917 and February 1918.
Vendegies	1	24km E of Cambrai. Bttn H.Q. during advance, October 1918.
Vendin lez Bethune	1	2km NW of Bethune. In billets, November 1917.
Vic sur Aisne	1	18km W of Soissons. A stopping place on the Retreat and where River Aisne crossed,1914.
Villers-Guislain	5	16km SSW of Cambrai. Advance, 1918.
Villiers St Genest	1	20km N of Meaux. Stopping place during retreat from Mons, 1914.
Vlamertinghe	5	3km W of Ypres. In huts, June 1915.
Vormezeel (Belgium)	6	5km S of Ypres. In trenches, March/April 1915.
Warlincourt	1	4km SW of Bapaume. Advance August '18.
Westhoek	3	6km E of Ypres. In lineAugust 1917.
Westoutre	13	6km SSE of Poperinge. In billets November/December 1914.
Windy Corner	3	At Cuinchy, near Bethune. October 1917. In Brigade support.
Wolfhoek	1	Near Locre. In transit, April 1918.
Wulverghem	13	3km W of Messines (now Mesen). In trenches May 1917. Centre for operations during Battle of Messines, June 1917.
Ypres	30	Rest during 1915.
Zillebeke	14	3km ESE of Ypres. October 1915.
Zillebeke Lake	3	Just to the NE of Zillebeke. In Brigade reserve, Sept. 1917.
Not Known	5	No entries in War Diary and nearest entries give no clues.

References

Ascoli, David	The Mons Star, Birlinn, Edinburgh, 2001.
British Commission for Military History	'Look to Your Front', Spellmont, 1999.
Cave, Nigel	Vimy Ridge (Battleground Europe Series), Leo Cooper 1996.
Congreave, Billy	Armageddon Road A V.C.'s Diary (ed. Terry Newman) Kimber, 1982.
Corns Cathryn & Hughes-Wilson, John	Blindfold and Alone, Cassell, 2001.
Corrigan, G.	Mud, Blood and Poppycock, Cassell, 2003.
Cumming H. R.	A Brigadier in France, Cape, 1922.
Edmonds Sir J. E. & others	History of the Great War - Military Operations France & Belgium (various dates). ('Official History')
Falls, C.	The History of the First Seven Battalions The Royal Irish Rifles In the Great War, Gale & Polden, 1925.
Farrer-Hockley, Anthony	Death of an Army, 1967.
Gaskell, C. H.	My Experiences in 1914 August to October . Ref. 99/55/1. Imperial War Museum Collection.
Gibson Tom	The Wiltshire Regiment (Famous Regiments Series), Leo Cooper, 1969.
Graves, Robert	Goodbye to All That, Cape, 1929.
Horsefall, J and Cave, N.	Mons 1914 (Battleground Europe series), Leo Cooper, 2000.
Kenrick, Lt. Col. N. C. E.	The Story of the Wiltshire Regiment, Gale & Polden, 1963.
Kincaid-Smith, Lt. Col. M.	The 25th Division in France and Flanders, Harrison, 1918.
Lucy, J. F.	There's a Devil in the Drum, Naval & Military Press, 1993.
Middlebrook, M.	The Kaiser's Battle, Allen Lane, 1978.

Mitchinson K. W.	Epehy (Battleground Europe Series) Leo Cooper 1998.
Mohan, T. G.	My War Diary. Ref. 80/28/1 Imperial War Museum Collection.
Oldham, Peter	Messines Ridge (Battleground Europe Series) Leo Cooper 1998.
Passingham, I.	Pillars of Fire: the Battle of Messines Ridge June 1917, Sutton, 1998.
Perry, H. G.	War Diary. Ref. 76/38/1 Imperial War Museum Collection
Sparling, R. A.	History of the 12th Service Battalion York & Lancaster Regiment, Sheffield, 1920.
Swayne, Lt. R.	Letters to parents. Ref. P163 Imperial War Museum Collection.
Terraine, J.	Mons. The Retreat to Victory, Wordsworth, Ware, 2002.
Wait, Capt. G. K.	Letters. GS1664 Liddle Collection, Brotherton Library, University of Leeds.
Westlake, Ray	Kitchener's Army, Spellmount, 1989.
White, Lt. A. J. S.	Lecture notes and recollections. GS1716 Liddle Collection, Brotherton Library, University of Leeds.
Official	Field Service Pocket Book (1914). David & Charles Reprint, 1971.